KidsRead Presents... AMAZING TALES

Voted BEST Middle and High School Product!

Make Your Own Volcano!

Tips From Microsoft Education!

Meet Collette!
Cookie Tycoon and Downs Advocate!

Inside:
- Games & Quizzes
- Recipes & Crafts
- STEM Activities
- How-to Videos
- Up-Close Inteviews

Build A Kid's

WHAT'S YOUR SUPERPOWER?

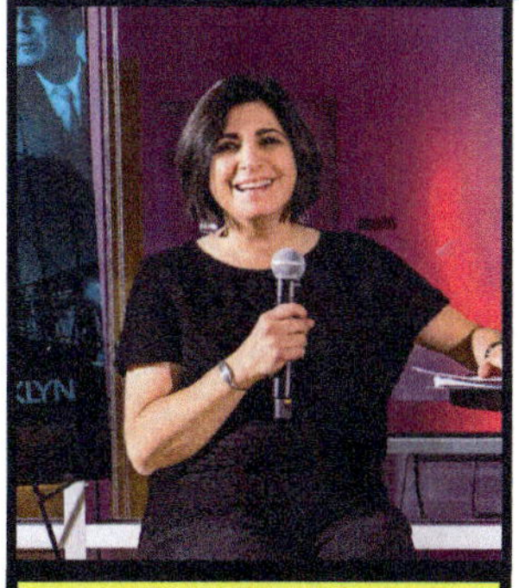

Connie Guglielmo — Editor-in-Chief of CNET

Brynjar — World Record Breaker

Neurodivergent Advocates

Siena — UN Young Leader and Author

Louis Henry Mitchell — Creative Director Sesame Workshop

WARNING: Amazing Tales Will Change Your Life!

Your world will never be the same.

You'll become addicted to our interactive activities, recipes, crafts, games, creative writing prompts, vocabulary supplements, video-tutorials, and **our secrets for success — in and out of school.** Through help with nutrition, sleep, and exercise - and asking good questions - you'll become an unstoppable lifelong learner, taking your future into your own hands.

Once you start, you'll see endless possibilities.

Amazing Tales will introduce you to creative careers you have never imagined — with **Sesame Workshop's** Creative Director of Character Design, **American Girl's** Executive Editor, the **LEGO Foundation's** VP of Learning Through Play, and more. **You'll even meet inspiring kids who are changing the world,** including Autistic Advocates: **UN Young Leader** Siena Castellon, and **World-Record Breaker,** Brynjar Karl. Through each feature, you'll practice crafting an original story.

Amazing Tales is empowering.

We feature **passionate** individuals with **creative minds, kind hearts,** and a **determination** to make a difference. Best of all: through Amazing Tales you'll see that...

MINDS LIKE YOURS HAVE THE POWER TO CHANGE THE WORLD!

Look for THIS tab at the start of each interactive activity ⟶

But Don't Take Our Word For It...

"**Superheroes and role models to help you love reading,** writing, and communicating, no matter what learning challenges you may face. Fun story starters, STEM activities, puzzles, and lessons learned from relatable kids who know what it's like to struggle in school and let you in on their secrets for success.

As a lifelong educator, **I'd be hard pressed to think of a more positive, proactive, compelling guide for young learners** who will be motivated to realize their dreams once they've gotten hooked on "Amazing Tales!" Parents, teachers, and administrators take note! This book is **a must-have for all the young people in your life.**

Dr. Julie M. Wood, Former Director of the Jeanne Chall Reading Lab, Harvard Graduate School of Education

"**An absolute revelation and revolution.** This book has everything in it that a young person with dyslexia will need to do life. There are strategies, activities, confidence boosters and personal stories shared by other young people! **It's accessible, engaging and beautifully put together!**

In short, this book is **a fantastic, practical resource** that young people (and their families) can dip in and out of as they move through school, further education and life together.

Dr. Helen Ross, Co-Vice Chair and Trustee, British Dyslexia Association

"**KidsRead2Kids has always found innovative and creative ways** to encourage kids to take charge of their own learning. With this book, they've taken it a step further, providing not only support, engaging characters and advice, but also the opportunity for readers to reflect and interact. **A must-read for kids (and caregivers) who want to feel empowered and understood!**

Amanda Morin, Neurodivergent Neurodiversity Consultant, author, speaker, and educator

"What a well-thought-out collection of stories, tips, and activities written by and for kids with learning differences. **The positive energy in this book can't help but make any child want to make the world a better place.** This is a must-have book to celebrate differences and recognize that we all have superpowers."

Marion Waldman, Founder/Executive Director, Teach My Kid to Read

Reading Outcomes

When you read Amazing Tales you will...

Become a confident, passionate, and independent lifelong learner

Get our personal secrets for success - in and out of school

Learn about creative career paths

Master must-have writing skills - including how-to design characters, research stories, and develop a pitch

Dream BIG through imaginative poetry

Practice new vocabulary words in a fun and engaging way

Meet inspiring mentors from across the globe

EMBRACE what makes you different ♥

WHAT'S YOUR SUPERPOWER?

Key tips for reading success:

Thanks to David Charrier, author of Master the Handpan.

1. Never compare yourself.

Harmful thinking:
"I will never be as good as my classmates."
"My brother learned in half the time."

Causes jealousy, low self-esteem, and self-sabotage

Remember that everyone learns differently and at their own pace. When you see someone else's success, offer congratulations, and leave it at that. Your learning is for you. Not for anyone else. Own it and enjoy it.

2. Be disciplined.

No one learns on the first try. **Discipline means staying dedicated and determined** even when things get hard — especially then. Consistency is key. Discipline helps you develop and stick to a routine, increase motivation, and ultimately, as your skill level progresses, will lead to more fun!

3. Slow down.

Building a strong foundation is key. It may be tempting to skip steps, but jumping ahead will only set you back in the future. Take it step-by-step with patience. Only move on when you feel confident. This is how you master a new skill for life. There is no hurry — take your time!

4. Accept that you will be frustrated.

But what is frustration? Frustration is the difference between where we are and where we want to go. We are frustrated because we are not there yet. When you feel frustrated, instead of quitting, admit it. **Channel it into MOTIVATION!**

meet the creators

Alana, Co-Founder of KidsRead2Kids, holds her BA in Creative Writing with a concentration in Education from Oberlin College. As a Business Scholar and Writing Associate, she trained in cross-disciplinary teaching practices and created original curriculum and activities. She worked in the community through the Writers in the Schools (WITS) Program at Langston Middle School, and as a local performing arts teacher. She later worked with SEEN Magazine, where she wrote five print and 30 online articles. She has dedicated the last few years to accessibility in education, by co-creating KidsRead2Kids Magazine (and serving as its Editor-in-Chief!), and speaking to international audiences.

Carol, Executive Director of KidsRead2Kids, holds an MBA and a BS in Economics, concentrated in Finance and Entrepreneurial Management from the Wharton School of Business, and a BS in Electrical and Systems Engineering from the University of Pennsylvania School of Engineering and Applied Science, where she was a Sharp Fellow and General Motors Scholar. She worked as an Associate Consultant for Bain & Company, as a Senior Consultant for Booz Allen Hamilton, and as an Adjunct Professor of Management for Northwood University. Carol was also the radio host of Entrepreneurial Life. **As a mother of five children with learning differences,** Carol has immersed herself in interactive ways to learn and grow. She helps educate across the globe, with lessons in mindfulness, exercise, nutrition, and positive play.

Lights... Camera... Reuben! An artist in print and on screen, and Chief Artistic Officer of KidsRead2Kids, he (literally!) brings learning to life. Reuben uses his gifts for fun and for good, and has been recognized as both a Point of Light and a Hershey Everyday Hero for his advocacy and commitment to bringing joy to kids around the world. When he isn't designing inspiring new creations, Reuben is an Early College Student, dual enrolled in an Associate of Applied Science program in Graphic Design while finishing high school. He's a busy guy! In fact, as a high school student, he served as founding president of KidsRead2Kids Book Club, where he brought reading, crafts, and positive self-esteem to struggling elementary school students.

Benjamin is an experiential learning designer turned property developer dedicated to creating fun and interactive educational experiences for kids (and adults!) of all ages. A former ballet dancer, engineer, and sculptor, and a lifelong explorer at heart, he very rarely stops moving! In his off time, his mind is on multi-sensory engagement, with special focus on accessibility through KidsRead2Kids, a children's literacy nonprofit managed in collaboration with his siblings. Benjamin holds his MEd in Experiential Learning and Development, his BSEd in Learning Design and Technology, and certification in school management and leadership.

Our founders!

Scan to Watch

our partners

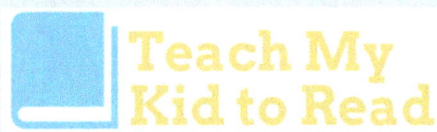  

THE CHARACTERS
(Meet Our Superheroes!)

ALANA: The Storyteller

Loves to imagine new worlds, feels deeply and with her whole heart, and dreams BIG... if only she could overcome her anxiety.

SUPERPOWER: Empathy

CAROL: Super-Mom

The ultimate mom: kind, caring, and a cheerleader for her children. She is determined to reach her goals, no matter how long it takes!

SUPERPOWER: Fearlessness

REUBEN: The Artist

A talented creator, designer, and day-dreamer, who can sketch anything from scratch... if only he could focus in class!

SUPERPOWER: Creativity

BENJAMIN: The Explorer

A natural people-person and brave adventurer, who can make friends with just about anyone... if only he could be in two places at once!

SUPERPOWER: Curiosity

JACOB: The Musician

A passionate singer-songwriter who faces struggle with courage and stays steadfast and determined: giving his ambitions everything he's got.

SUPERPOWER: Bravery

NOW IT'S YOUR TURN!

What kind of hero are you?

- [ ]
- [ ]
- [ ]
- [ ]
- [ ]
- [ ]

SELF-PORTRAIT

Dear Readers,

When Jacob and I first imagined KidsRead2Kids, we were 13 and 15 years old. I was an overly excited, frizzy-haired, dork of a sophomore; he was collected and calm, and way too cool to be in eighth grade *(in my eyes anyway...)*.

We were in different places in our lives, but our problem was the same: no matter where we went, we never felt like we belonged.

You see, underneath his cool exterior, Jacob was struggling with an invisible disability. Dyslexia impacted his life in all ways, from his grades in school to his energy level, to his perception of himself.

Day after day, he would come home with pressure-ridden shoulders, feeling defeated and alone. But little did he know, there were countless other kids — just like him.

According to Understood.org, 1 in 5 children in the US learn differently, yet only 30 percent of educators feel confident to teach them — leaving their future completely in the hands of their parents. Without access to support and resources, these kids risk repeating a grade, facing school suspension, or not finishing school at all. Many kids with undiagnosed learning disabilities also struggle with their self-esteem.

Left to fend for themselves, they are likely to feel less capable than their classmates. Jacob certainly felt that way.

As for me? I grew up with Selective Mutism. Wide-eyed and careful, I thought of every possible consequence before making decisions *(I still do...)*. While I could find comfort at home, my voice ended there. Even the simplest things such as keeping eye contact or raising my hand in class seemed impossible. At school, I would hold my breath and pray to be skipped over at attendance. When the teacher called my name, the inevitable 'she's not here,' was soon to follow.

Though I was always surrounded by people who loved me, I felt alone; almost like I didn't matter.

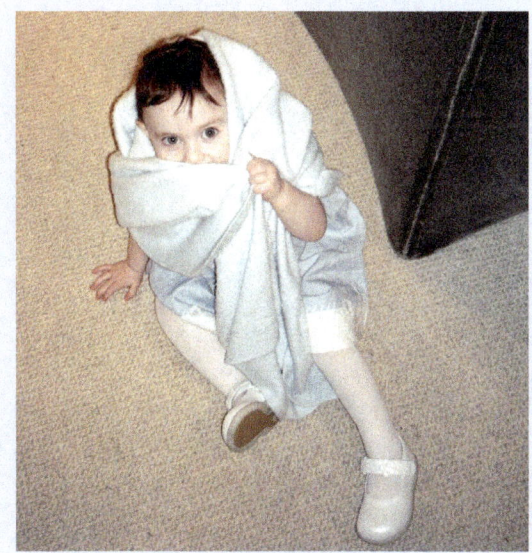

Hiding from the paparazzi.

My superheroes!

Even as a sophomore, I was still that same girl that avoided attention like the plague; whose worst-case scenario was having nothing worthy to say.

Now, my condition is rare, impacting less than one percent of the US *(that's me!)*, according to the National Center for Rare Disorders. But anxiety and depression affect millions. Further, the Learning Disabilities Association of America states that children with learning disabilities are prone to chronic depression.

But something stopped me from falling into that deep, dark abyss: I had a family with the time and resources to support me. Without them, I would not be who I am today. My mother, as an undiagnosed dyslexic, understood how we felt and did everything she could to help.

As you'll read in her Mom2Mom column, she went to the moon and back to ensure our success.

While my father went a different route, dedicating his time in bedtime stories. His readings of classics like Anne of Green Gables provided us not only with role models but also with a needed escape from the outside world. Our father brought classic novels to life, without us having to decode the words. Instead, we would simply close our eyes and imagine Prince Edward Island and its lovable characters as if they were real before us. Night after night, I grew fond of spirited, red-headed Anne, wishing that for once, I could be as brave.

And, like all epiphanies, one day Jacob and I just knew: it was time to make a change.

So, in 2016, we founded a place where we could all belong, no matter our difference. We called it KidsRead2Kids.

Everyone deserves to experience the magic of reading and to know that they are not alone. Our goal is to share that joy with the world.

Today, we've recorded 17 classic novels read by our team of high school volunteers; we've filmed a range of decodable chapter books for early learners; and recently, we published our lesson plans to beloved novels, Peter Pan and Anne of Green Gables. We film all of our books chapter by chapter so that anyone can listen and learn at their own pace. Our resources have reached struggling readers, parents, teachers, and libraries worldwide. **But we are far from done**.

Our very first attempt at filming a video!

You're never truly alone with a Reading Bear by your side!

Too many children feel alone in their struggles, unknowing that there is a community of learners like them. Let's change that. With our book, *Amazing Tales*, we are taking our mission one step further by introducing real role models across the world.

Here, we share our best tips for living a healthy, happy, and confident life — in and out of school. Meet inspiring changemakers, renowned experts, and fascinating kids who embrace their differences. Our book is full of incredible people with varying career paths from Muppeteer Bruce Lanoil to American Girl's Executive Editor, Jennifer Hirsch, to Sesame Workshop's Creative Director of Character Design!

Head to the Kids Corner and you'll find UN Young Leader and Autism Advocate Siena Castellon and Brynjar Karl, who broke a world record with nothing but Legos.

Our features are passionate individuals with creative minds, kind hearts, and a determination to make a difference. Day by day, these role models are changing the world — and best of all? They are just like you.

Sincerely,
Alana Blumenstein
**Co-Founder and Editor-in-Chief
KidsRead2Kids**

TABLE OF

Tips From Us

- **19** — Questions From Our Readers + What I Wish I Knew About My Struggles
- **24** — Active Listening Explained + 7 Ways to Get Started
- **30** — Three Steps Towards a Balanced Life + **Worksheet:** Create Your Own Breakfast Menu
- **46** — Tips & Tricks to Help You Focus + **Worksheet:** Building Healthy Habits
- **50** — How I Learned to Raise My Hand In Class + **Worksheet:** Finding Your Voice
- **56** — What's My Superpower? Neurodivergent Heroes Today and In History

The Kids Corner

- **65** — Meet Our Readers (Steven, Aarav, Aaralyn and Karter!) + **QUIZ:** Which Peter Pan Character Are You?
- **78** — Brynjar Karl Broke a World Record with Nothing But Legos
- **84** — UN Young Leader Siena Castellon Celebrates Neurodiversity
- **91** — **Interactive Worksheet:** Our Next Feature is YOU!

CONTENTS

96 — Ready. Set. STEM! **CRAFT:** Make your own play-dough and exploding volcano!

98 — Our Favorite Treats (Fun snacks, smoothies, and more!) **+ RECIPE:** Make Protein Bites with Us!

102 — Our Personal Favorite Educational Apps For School Success

104 — We're Going on a Bear Hunt **+ CRAFT:** Make Your Own Bear-Noculars!

109 — The Reading Nest: Literature Galore! **+ QUIZ:** What Kind of Reader Are You? **+ Worksheet:** Write Your Own Poetry!

131 — Meet Sesame Workshop's Louis Henry Mitchell **+ Worksheet:** Character Design - The "WHO"

140 — Meet American Girl's Executive Editor Jennifer Hirsch **+ Worksheet:** Story Ingredients **+ QUIZ:** Are You a Kit or a Ruthie?

152 — Meet Muppeteer Bruce Lanoil **+ Worksheet:** Character Appearance **+ CRAFT:** Make Mini Monster Puppets!

158 — Meet LEGO Foundation's VP Bo Stjerne Thomsen **+ Worksheet:** Design Your World

164 — Meet Connie Guglielmo, Editor-in-Chief of CNET **+ Worksheet:** Research Like a Reporter

Expert Advice

172 — Meet Amanda Gummer of Dr. Gummer's Good Play Guide + **Worksheet:** Bring Your Story to Life

178 — Meet Cookie-preneur and Downs Advocate Collette Divitto + **Worksheet:** Story Lessons

181 — Meet Executive Producer James Longman + **Worksheet:** From Page to Screen - Write Your Pitch

189 — Surviving School with Mike Tholfsen From Microsoft Education

192 — The Benefits of Reading Aloud by Literacy Expert Faith Borkowsky

196 — Keep Calm and Conference On by Neurodiveristy Expert Amanda Morin

201 — Welcome to Mom2Mom: Meet Our Mom, Carol! + The Role of Teachers and Parents

206 — Dad2Dad with Jordan Levin: On Growing Up Deaf and ADHD

210 — Five tips to help your dyslexic child with homework by Nicole Holcomb

211 — **Vocabulary Supplement:** Find each word, definition, and corresponding example here.

Mom2Mom (and Dad!)

Amazing Tales
Hunt for the answers as you read!

Psst... answer key on page 212!

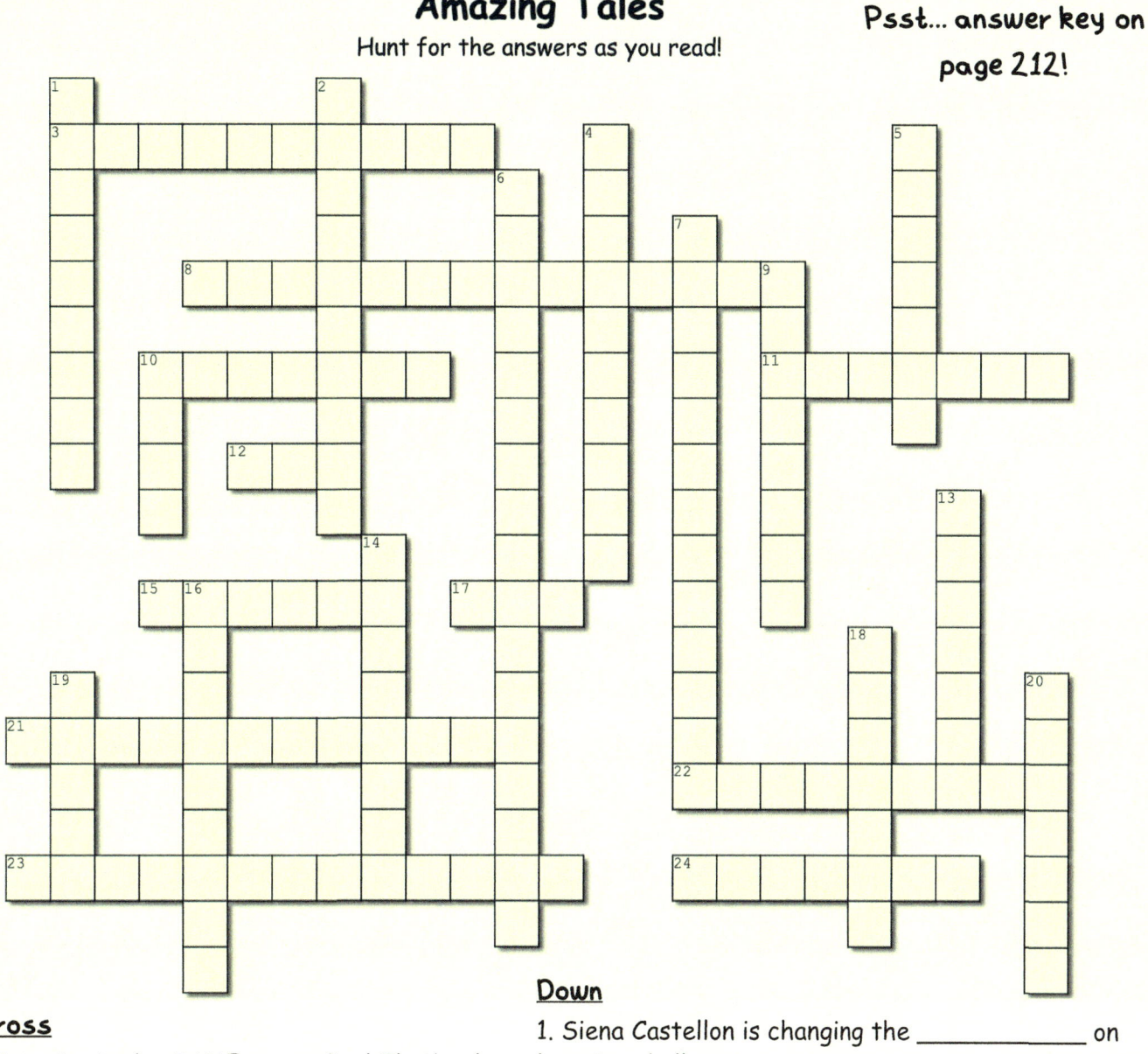

Across

3. Listening is the SAME as reading! That's why we love listening to _____. (Hint: Check Questions From Our Readers)
8. What is Jacob's favorite book?
10. Bruce Lanoil plays _____ for a living.
11. What is Alana's superpower?
12. According to American Girl's Jennifer Hirsch, all stories have a beginning, middle, and end. Or, an _____.
15. In Tips From Us, we encourage _____ listening.
17. How many flavors does Collette's cookie company have?
21. For those struggling to read, try _____, low-level books.
22. Where is Aarav from?
23. Who is Louis Henry Mitchell's favorite Sesame Street Muppet?
24. Literacy expert Faith Borkowsky emphasizes the importance of _____ aloud.

Down

1. Siena Castellon is changing the _____ on learning challenges.
2. Our mission is to bring the joy, _____, and curiosity back to all readers.
4. Bo Stjerne Thomsen is the VP of Learning Through Play at the LEGO _____.
5. What makes you different makes you _____.
6. What is Benjamin's favorite book?
7. What is our nonprofit called?
9. To live a balanced life, we must focus on diet, sleep, and _____.
10. Amanda Gummer credits _____ for her success.
13. What exploding craft do we make in Ready. Set. STEM?
14. What book does our volunteer Steven read?
16. What is Benjamin's superpower?
18. What record-breaking LEGO ship did Brynjar build?
19. Mike Tholfsen of Microsoft Education loves giving his _____ tips.
20. Where is Brynjar from?

Tips From Us

Dear KidsRead2Kids,

My name is Lexi, I'm in 6th grade, and I struggle with dyslexia. I'm really embarrassed because I read slower than my classmates. What can I do to become a better reader?

Lexi, New York

Hi Lexi,

What a great question! One of the reasons we started KidsRead2Kids was to give others a safe place to improve their active listening skills while introducing them to the world of audio-books.

Audio-books are a great way to improve our reading skills. Many people don't know that **listening is the SAME as reading!** It's like walking versus driving: the destination is the same, no matter how we get there.

My brother Jacob uses audio-books all the time - whether he is listening to his textbooks or enjoying a book before bed.

We suggest **high-interest, low-level books.** Literacy skills are known to improve when we read what we enjoy. **If we are drawn to a story, we are more likely to stick with it.**

So, **find books based on your current interests,** whether that is science, sports, mystery, or graphic novels. My younger brother Reuben loves comic books. Don't worry if the book seems too difficult to read. You can always start with the audio-book.

Decodable chapter books are also a wonderful way of learning to read. These books are specifically designed to help new readers. Some great ones for young readers include Dog on the Log Books, Spire Decodable Readers, Primary Phonics, and BOB Books. We even have some on our website!

Most importantly, **believe in your abilities.** It may take a little longer, but you will learn. The most important thing is to find a love of reading. If your have that, you will grow to be a lifelong learner.

Now you're ready to start practicing!

On our website, we offer a number of video-audiobooks of abridged classic novels, as well as a range of decodable chapter books. Pick your favorite story, press play, and enjoy!

In between chapters, put your active listening skills to the test with our lesson Plans! Currently, our offerings include Peter Pan and Anne of Green Gables.

We would love to hear from you. Please share your stories on how you listen best! Reach out anytime at info@kidsread2kids.com.

Website: KidsRead2Kids.com/classic-novels

YouTube: KidsRead2Kids

Connect with Us!

Reading...

...lets me travel to awesome places in my imagination.
...takes me on new adventures without ever leaving my room.
...helps me read better, read faster, and do better in school.
... helps me become an Active Listener
...inspires me to learn something new and to be anything I want.

...expands your world, one book at a time.

Meet Felix: Our Worry Box
©2021-2024 KidsRead2Kids

INTRODUCING...
KIDSREAD2KIDS WORD JAR
AND
STORY STARTERS

©2023 KidsRead2Kids

CLICK HERE TO WATCH!

"It's the perfect interactive tool to help build your child's vocabulary. I love all the elements of this product. It has everything to help your child either play alone or with friends. I highly recommend it!"

"I can tell everything included was very well thought out in helping your child create wonderful stories from their imagination."

"I really love this educational storytelling tool. I presented it to my daughter at the review and she began creating her own story right away. Wonderful product!"

Families LOVE our Word Jar!

"What I wish I knew about my 🏳️‍🌈 struggles..." 🏳️‍🌈

Jacob: I wish I knew that dyslexia didn't make me less-than my classmates. When I was younger, I thought I was stupid because I couldn't read. Now, I know dyslexia makes me learn differently, and that's not a bad thing.

Reuben: I wish I knew that showing symptoms of ADHD didn't make me lazy or a bad person. I used to fidget and doodle A LOT in class, and my teachers would get frustrated with me. I still do, but now I'm able to focus more on my strengths.

Alana: I wish I knew that everyone's voice matters: even mine. When I was little, I used to hold my breath in class and try not to make a sound. Now, I share my struggles openly so that others feel less alone.

A list of things you should know when you're diagnosed.

1. You are NOT alone.

Take it from us - there are people around the globe with struggles just like your own.

2. There are tools that can help you.

Utilize the resources available to you. (Head to the page 102 for our favorite apps!) for our favorite apps!)

3. Our struggles give us valuable strengths.

We are grateful for our learning disabilities. They've made us who we are.

4. What makes you different makes you special.

Regardless of your struggles, you are AWESOME. We wouldn't change a thing.

Active Listening Explained: 7 Ways to Get Started!

Active Listening is a key tool in and out of school. However, it's not formally taught and can be difficult to learn. Here's how we got started!

By KidsRead2Kids Team

Have you ever felt lost during class? Do you have a hard time listening to others? Many people don't know **there is a difference between hearing and listening**.

We hear sounds all day. We are born with that ability. But being an Active Listener is a skill we must develop.

So, what is Active Listening?

Active Listening is the ability to process what we have heard and remember what we have learned.

To describe the difference between *hearing* and *listening*, we at KidsRead2Kids use the phrase, "I hear you but I'm not listening." This signals that **although we have heard the speaker, we have not processed the information**. Therefore, we cannot remember it later.

Unfortunately, active listening techniques are not taught in school. Listening, like reading, is one of the most important skills you will ever have. You will need to listen in school, at work, and in life.

If you are struggling, please do not worry. It is nothing to be ashamed of. Learning to actively listen can be very challenging — especially with a learning difference.

Dyslexia, ADHD, and other processing delays make it even harder to pay attention. As we know, when we struggle to **focus**, we struggle to **learn**.

That's why we have designed our program specifically to help you improve your listening skills. The more you practice, the stronger you will become.

No matter what, always remember that you are not alone. We've been there, too.

So, here are our top tips for getting started. These steps helped us, and we hope they help you.

1. Find a quiet place to listen.

"Personally, I cannot focus when I'm in a noisy space," our co-founder Alana says. "I get easily distracted, so I like to find a cozy, quiet spot to study."

2. Choose a relaxing time of the day (such as bedtime).

"Sometimes when I try to read at a very busy time of day, it's hard for me to focus," Reuben (14) says. "When I come back to it later, or at night, it's a lot easier to get into it."

3. Make eye contact with your reader.

"When I'm in class listening to a lecture, it's easier to stay focused and engaged when I'm actually making eye contact with my teacher," our sister Julia explains.

4. Close your eyes and imagine the story as it is read.

"You know you understand a story when you can picture it in your mind," our mom Carol shares.

5. Practice staying completely present and engaged with the story.

To be fully engaged, Julia likes to start with her favorite stories. "I would start with something I'm interested in and then move on to something more complicated," Julia (16) says. When she's in class, Julia once again points out the importance of eye contact.

> "It's harder to listen when I'm not interested but focusing on my teachers allows me to hear what they're saying and interpret it in my own way."

6. Summarize the story to yourself out loud after each chapter.

"Whenever I'm struggling to remember or process information, I try to teach it to myself," Alana (20) says. "Talking out loud always helps me."

7. Listen to the chapter again. See how much you remember from the first time!

"When you're learning, it's so important to listen to things more than once," Alana shares. "When I listen again, I often hear things that I missed the first time."

Everybody is a **GENIUS**.

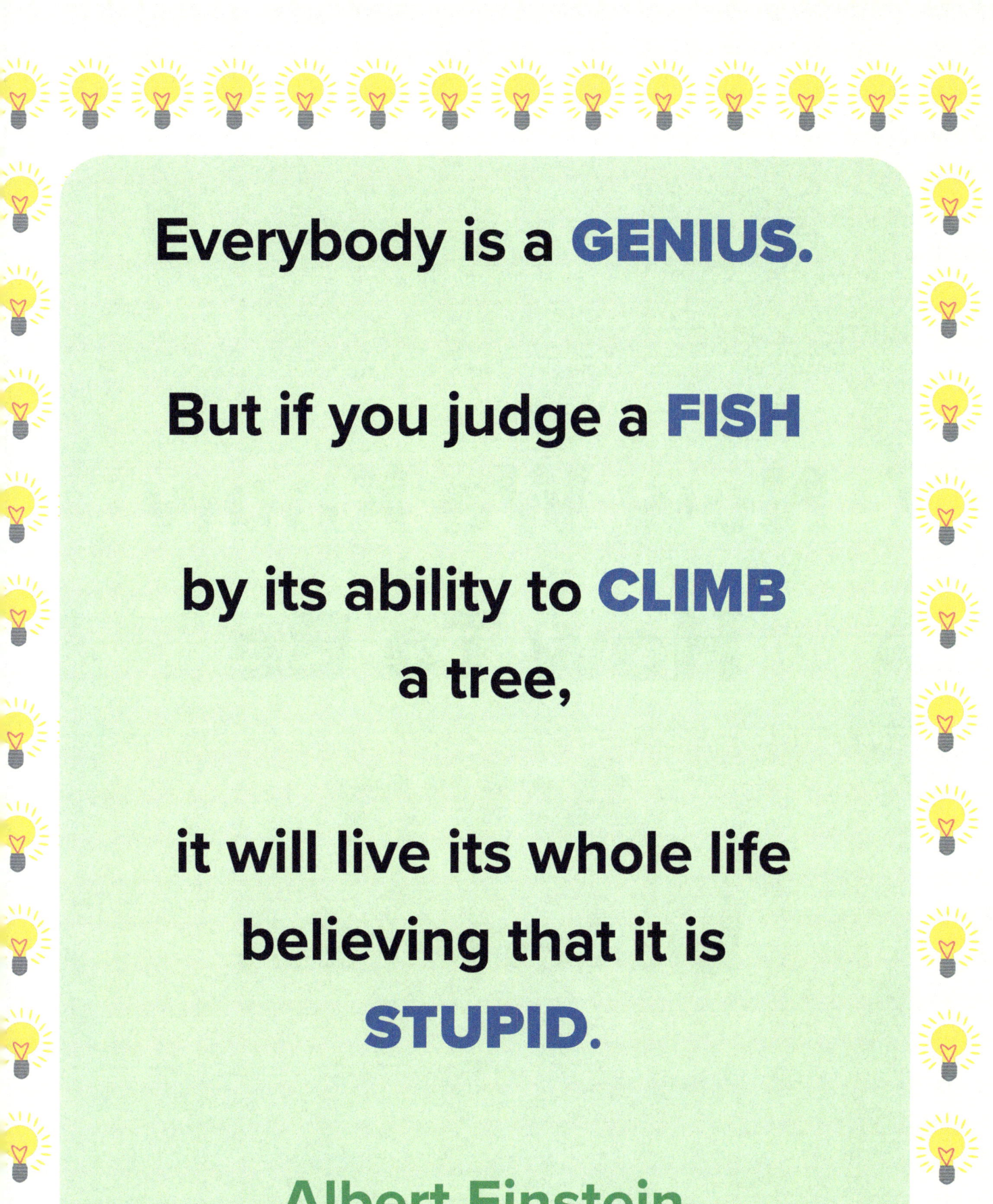

But if you judge a **FISH**

by its ability to **CLIMB**
a tree,

it will live its whole life
believing that it is
STUPID.

Albert Einstein

Now We Know How To Be Active Listeners...

... BUT learning is not just what happens IN the classroom...

Learning is what happens OUT of the classroom, too.

Three Steps Toward a Balanced Life:

1. Diet
2. Exercise
3. Sleep

*Make sure to talk to your parent before making any changes!

1 Change Your Diet, Change Your World

DID YOU KNOW?

What you eat affects your productivity. Food has a direct impact on your ability to focus, to use your memory, and even just to think!

WHAT IS NUTRITION?

Nutrition is everything that you eat or drink. Your body uses nutrients from food to stay energized, healthy, and strong.

Our Checklist for Every Meal:

- ☐ Protein
- ☐ Carbohydrates
- ☐ Healthy Fats

DID YOU KNOW?

Eating well-balanced meals will not only make you feel better, but will also make your life - in and out of school - so much easier.

Let's Break It Down

*Some may overlap!

Protein

Lean meats (ex: chicken, turkey, etc.), dairy (ex: milk, cheese, yogurt, etc.) fish (salmon, tuna, halibut, etc.), eggs, beans, quinoa, lentils, peas, nuts, protein powders, and more!

Carbohydrates

Whole grains, vegetables, fruit, beans, bread, rice, potatoes, and more!

Healthy Fats

Avocado, olive oil, nuts, egg yolk, dairy, and more!

To learn more about your nutrition, visit ChooseMyPlate.Gov

When you improve your nutrition...

...you sleep soundly

...you wake up energized

...you balance your mood

...you improve your WORLD!

STEP ONE: Start the Day Off Strong

Breakfast is the most important meal of the day - and for good reason.

By KidsRead2Kids Team

Do you ever feel tired in the morning? Does no amount of sleep feel like enough? Do you find it almost impossible to stay focused?

Well... do you eat breakfast?

Think about it. We sleep for several hours at night (around 9-11 hours if we stick to a good bedtime - see more on page 42). That's a lot of time to go without food.

That's why it's super important to break your fast and make some time for breakfast.

Breakfast gives your body energy to start a new day.

Think of it as a jump start. Breakfast is the fuel our minds and bodies need to take on the day.

We expect a lot from ourselves. From paying attention in class to hanging out with friends to participating in extra-curricular activities; it can feel endless.

So, even if you don't **feel** hungry, **your body needs breakfast** to stay healthy, energized, and strong.

What Will I Eat For Breakfast?

CARBOHYDRATE
Whole-grain breads, cereals, muffins, oatmeal & fruit

PROTEIN
Eggs, milk, yogurt, fish, turkey bacon or sausage, etc.

FAT
Avocado, yogurt, eggs, fish, olive oil

Balanced Meal Examples:
- Avocado toast with egg and fruit
- Peanut butter smoothie
(check out page 100 for our recipe!)
- Steel cut oats with blueberries
- Yogurt parfait

My Breakfast Menu

Your Turn!

GET CREATIVE! Create three meal options, using at least one protein, carbohydrate, and healthy fat for a balanced breakfast.

2   More Exercise = More Energy

DID YOU KNOW?

Exercise not only strengthens you physically, but also mentally. The more active you are, the more energy you have, increasing your ability to focus and retain new information.

HAPPINESS IS KEY.

Any kind of movement is exercise, from simply taking a walk outside to having a dance party in your bedroom!

MOVE FOR MENTAL HEALTH.

When we exercise, our bodies grow stronger, and our minds become calmer and less anxious.

WALKING: Get fresh air and blow off steam by taking a nice walk. Your mind will thank you later!

TIP FROM US:
Take a deep breath and count to ten. As you walk, appreciate the world around you. Name five things you love about your path.

Other Exercise Options

Circle 3 or more you'd like to explore.

- DANCE
- BASKETBALL
- TRACK & FIELD
- GYMNASTICS
- BASEBALL / SOFTBALL
- FIGURE SKATING
- MARTIAL ARTS
- HOCKEY

TENNIS	SOCCER
CHEERLEADING	FOOTBALL
ARCHERY	YOGA
SWIMMING	CYCLING
VOLLEYBALL	(add your own)

3 Quality Sleep, Quality Life

DID YOU KNOW?

It isn't just how much sleep you get, it's the quality of your sleep too! How you sleep directly impacts your success in school. In fact, sleep helps both learning and memory.

A NEW PERSPECTIVE

Lets face it: school is tiring. Your mind works hard throughout the day - especially if you have a learning disability. Make sure to make time to rest and refresh: a reasonable bedtime means more fun tomorrow!

To learn more about your sleep, visit NIH.Gov

BEDTIME ISN'T JUST FOR KIDS

Going to bed at the same time each night helps your body know when it's time to rest.

Setting a schedule, also called your circadian rhythm, not only makes sleeping easier, it improves the quality!

BUT I'M TOO OLD FOR BEDTIME!

You don't outgrow your bedtime, you just get old enough to manage it yourself! Aim for 9-11 hours of sleep: the perfect amount to prep your mind for a full school day.

Tip: Just 15 minutes of morning sunlight can help regulate your circadian rhythm.

"Now, we've learned how to eat, exercise, and sleep…"

"Which means we can FOCUS and gain confidence."

You are **BRAVER** than you believe, **STRONGER** than you seem, and **SMARTER** than you think.

Christopher Robin

Tips and tricks to help you focus!

Whether you're a daydreamer or a fidgeter, here's some tips to help you stay alert and focused.

By KidsRead2Kids Team

Do you have trouble sitting still? Are you easily distracted? Staying focused for long periods of time can be exhausting for anyone.

Don't be hard on yourself: if it seems impossible to pay attention, it isn't because you're not trying. Take it from us—as a family with learning differences, we've all had our struggles.

That's why we've put together our favorite tips and tricks!

1. Exercise, exercise, exercise!

Did you know exercising improves focus? Moving your body motivates your brain and helps you think and learn better! It's also a great release of stress.

"I cannot think or focus without exercise," Reuben says. "I try to go to the gym and take walks as much as I can."

Many people don't realize the benefits of simply walking. "Walking is a great way to exercise," Alana explains. "It's easy, requires no tools, and gives you some fresh air!"

Tip: Join a sports or dance team, take a walk, go bike riding... the possibilities are endless! Try something **fun** that gets your body moving.

2. Find YOUR reading nest.

We personally cannot focus unless we're cozy. Find a spot in your school or house where you feel comfortable and at-ease.

Everyone's brains work differently. Some work better with company, and others need complete quiet and privacy.

3. Turn off all electronics.

Unless they are a learning-related tool, turn off your screens. Keep your focus on your current assignment and do your best to cut out all other possible disruptions.

Tip: Stay away from anything that may tempt you to lose focus (computers, phones, televisions, etc.). Put it in a drawer or in a separate room.

4. Take timed breaks.

Your brain can get tired after working too long, so make sure to come up for air every once in a while! Set a timer so you don't lose track of time.

Tip: During your break, get up and stretch. Take a lap around the room. This will get your blood flowing!

5. Eat a balanced, healthy diet.

Eating healthy can make a world of difference. This doesn't mean that you have to give up dessert. We suggest an "everything in moderation" lifestyle.

Eating the right foods can boost your productivity and make it easier to stay focused. Head to page 98 for our favorite after-school snack! (It's hard to focus on an empty stomach...)

6. Get enough sleep.

Getting the right amount of sleep is key to being in focus. Remember: if you're tired, your brain will be too. Give yourself the rest you need to maintain your energy.

Tip: Shut off screens an hour before bedtime. Give yourself time to take deep breaths and unwind.

7. Stay hydrated.

When you're dehydrated, you're likely to get headaches, have poor concentration, and have trouble with your short-term memory.

Tip: Keep a water bottle close-by while you work.

> In time, these lifestyle changes will make a difference. Just keep trying and believe in yourself!

Your Turn!

Building Healthy Habits

1. How will you exercise? (ex: daily walks, sports team, etc.)

2. Describe your reading nest! Where is it located? What does it look like? How does it make you feel?

3 & 4. Where will you store your electronics? How often will you take breaks?

5. What healthy foods will you eat? (We love our peanut butter protein bites!)

6. How many hours will you sleep at night? Set an ideal bedtime and wake-up time.

7. How will you stay hydrated? (We love drinking tea!)

Congratulations! You are one step closer towards becoming your strongest self!

How I Learned to Raise My Hand In Class:

Advice From Someone Who's Been There, Too

To those of you who are afraid to participate in class, you are not alone. That's why I've included a list on ways to gain confidence in yourself—and your voice.

By Alana Blumenstein

It's no secret that I was extremely shy as a child. My Selective Mutism stopped me from raising my voice to anyone - even my own extended family. Wrecked with anxiety, I hid from everything and everyone.

My fear of speaking extended to school, too. At night, I would lay awake with anxiety. My stomach would cramp with dread. My breathing would quicken involuntarily.

> In class, I wanted to disappear. I hunched down into my seat and tried to become invisible.

I could not even raise my voice at morning attendance. When my name was called, I would sit quietly and wait to be noticed. Often, half the class would pass before I was marked as present.

My biggest worry was that my teacher would call on me. In my mind, speaking up could only end one way: school-wide humiliation.

I remember planning out my answers ahead of time, just in case the dreaded worst-case scenario occurred.

> Though I still get nervous speaking in front of others, I now push myself to do it anyways.

> Here are the 7 ways I've learned to gain confidence in myself—and my voice. And soon, you will too!

1. Approach your teacher before or after class.

One of the first things I *always, always, always* recommend is getting to know your teacher outside of class.

Speaking to your teacher privately can help you establish a relationship, which will in turn boost your confidence. **Your teachers are your advocates** - they are here for your success.

But, teachers aren't mind-readers! Being honest about your struggles will not only show that you care, but will also show them how to best support you.

If confiding your worries aloud seems intimidating, write your thoughts down. Or send your teacher a quick email! It's okay if in-person conversation doesn't happen right away. As a bonus, seeing your worries written out can be calming.

2. Ask your questions privately first.

My biggest fear used to be asking questions. For the longest time, I worried that voicing my inner thoughts would make me sound stupid.

But... no question is stupid!

Everyone always says that, but testing out my questions in a safe and private environment made me realize how true it really is. No matter what your question is, it's likely someone else in your class is thinking that same thing.

3. Take charge in your daily life.

For example, practice ordering food for your family over the phone or in person at a restaurant. When ordering, be confident, and don't be afraid to ask any questions you have about the menu.

Whenever you have a question, ask it!

Whether you're looking for something in a grocery store or are trying on clothes in a boutique, there are plenty of opportunities to push yourself in daily life.

4. Discover your unique strengths.

Are you creative, imaginative, or a problem-solver? Are you musical, artistic, or an original thinker? Everyone has their own set of talents and strengths. Sometimes, all it takes is finding yours.

Try thinking about what comes easy to you. **Remember, everyone learns differently, and no one is perfect at everything.** So, what makes *you* shine?

For me, I'm a creative, passionate, people person. I love writing, having deep conversations, and expressing myself creatively. Which leads me to my next point...

5. Find a team-oriented passion.

Working in teams is a great way to practice using your voice. Once you've found your unique talents, it's time to find a team that compliments those things.

If you are a good performer, audition for the school musical. If you love finding patterns, join the robotics team. If you are a writer, like me, report for the school newspaper.

Take note of the value you add to your team. Your voice *does* matter, and your contributions are important!

6. Push yourself out of your comfort zone.

You're never going to grow if you don't give yourself a little push! Try an extracurricular activity that forces you to confront your fears - even if it doesn't match your current skill-set.

When I was younger, I took Russian Ballet lessons. I was the worst in the class! But it didn't matter, because every time I made a mistake, I was supported by my company.

Dance, theater, and sports are all great options. Even if you don't make it, you'll know that you tried. And, more importantly, once you've seen the dreaded "worst-case scenario," you'll realize that it isn't as scary as you expected.

7. Raise your hand.

Now, it's time to face your fears! There is no one solution that is going to make you feel more comfortable in class. But, if you stay determined, keep a positive mindset, and try your best, there is nothing you can't do.

Always remember to be kind to yourself. Your thoughts and opinions are just as valuable as anyone else's. YOU matter, and your voice does too.

Your Turn!

Things I'm good at...

Ex: Writing, Theater

Team Oriented Passions

Ex: Newspaper, Musical

Things I'd like to try...

Ex: Softball, Chemistry, anything!

Questions I'm afraid to ask...

Hint: show this to your teacher!

Still anxious? That's okay! Email your questions to us at info@kidsread2kids.com

Why fit in when you were born to STAND OUT?

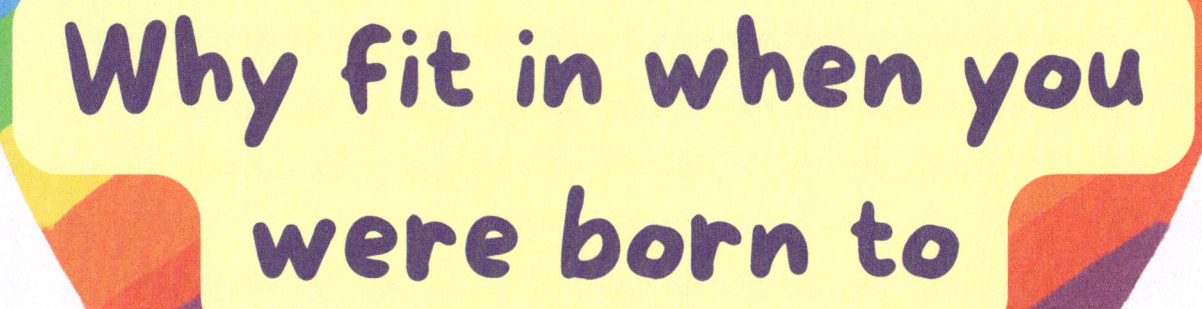

Dr. Seuss

WHAT'S MY SUPERPOWER?

Not all superheroes wear capes.

DID YOU KNOW?

Learning disabilities come with their fair share of struggles, but they also empower us with wonderful strengths. Our experience with our flaws give us the best gift of all: empathy.

DYSLEXIA:

Dyslexics see the world differently and bring a new perspective. They are often inventive, out-of-the-box, big picture thinkers with a talent for problem solving and spotting patterns.

Fun fact: Our Co-Founder Jacob is dyslexic! At Ross Business School, he studies consulting, where he spots trends in data and tackles hard problems every day.

ADHD:

People with ADHD are enthusiastic and sensitive, which makes them great friends. They are filled with creative ideas, and can hyper-focus on their passions.

Fun fact: Our Co-Founder Reuben has ADHD! As a high school student, he is in an Associates Program for Graphic Design, where he uses his creativity to create incredible art.

Dysgraphia:

Because dysgraphics have difficulty writing by hand, they can command attention using their voices. They are very entertaining and powerful storytellers.

Fun fact: Our Co-Founder Alana has dysgraphia! She loves telling stories and making people laugh, which makes her a great public speaker!

Neurodivergent Heroes

Real and Imaginary

PART ONE - Let's take a look at history!

Albert Einstein - Dyslexia

One of the most influential physicists of all time! His theory on relativity helps us understand space, time, gravity, and the universe.

Alexander Graham Bell - ADHD

This Scottish scientist and engineer was the inventor of the telephone!

Emily Dickinson - Autism Spectrum Disorder

A revolutionary American poet. Many experts believe this reclusive writer was on the spectrum.

PART TWO - Famous figures today

Steven Spielberg - Dyslexia

One of the most successful film directors in history. His long list of movies include Jaws, ET: Extra Terrestrial, Jurassic Park, and West Side Story!

Simone Biles - ADHD

This gymnast has won seven Olympic medals and is one of the most awarded athletes in American history.

Selena Gomez - Anxiety, Depression, & Bipolar Disorder

This former Disney star, musician, and businesswoman speaks openly about her struggles with mental health.

PART THREE - Fictional characters

Percy Jackson - Dyslexia

Many demigods in The Lightning Thief by Rick Riordan have dyslexia. Their brains are wired to read Ancient Greek, not English! Though Percy struggled in school, he thrived when he found others like him.

Anne Shirley - Possible ADHD

Many experts believe that Anne of Green Gables's imaginative, energetic spirit could stem from ADHD. Anne is a daydreamer, deeply sensitive, and can be a bit impulsive. Her passion for words and positive outlook inspires us all.

"If you're always trying to be **NORMAL** you will never know how **AMAZING** you can be."

— Maya Angelou 🏳️‍🌈

My Vocabulary

Learning words can be FUN!

Together, let's meet fascinating people - and hunt for our favorite words! Before we begin, here are four types of words to look for:

NOUN	People, places, or things	**Examples**: Man, woman, teacher, home, beach, school, car, food, etc.
VERB	An action word Hint! "To ____"	**Examples**: Run, walk, dance, hike, swim, jump, climb, call, cheer, etc.
ADJECTIVE	A descriptive word Hint! "Are/am/is ____"	**Examples**: Nice, mean, beautiful, friendly, clever, brave, athletic, etc.
ADVERB	A word that changes feeling, amount, or time in a sentence!	**Examples**: Quickly, beautifully, cheerfully, very, always, already, almost, etc.

The word hunt starts NOW!

*Find all definitions beginning on page 213.

VOCABULARY
Superpower Edition!

Empathy	**NOUN** — The ability to understand another's feelings and point-of-view	Tip: Put yourself in their shoes! How would YOU feel you were them?
Fearless	**ADJECTIVE** — Not afraid of anything; bold and courageous	Tip: Try something out of your comfort zone (ex: audition for the school play!)
Creative	**ADJECTIVE** — Able to imagine or design original ideas	Tip: Find a passion and CREATE! Draw, paint, write, build... the possibilities are endless!
Curious	**ADJECTIVE** — A strong desire to learn or know something	Tip: Make a habit of asking questions: you'll be surprised at what you learn!
Bravely	**ADVERB** — Facing obstacles head-on and with courage	Tip: Stay determined, hold onto your passions, and stand up for what you believe in.

The Kids Corner

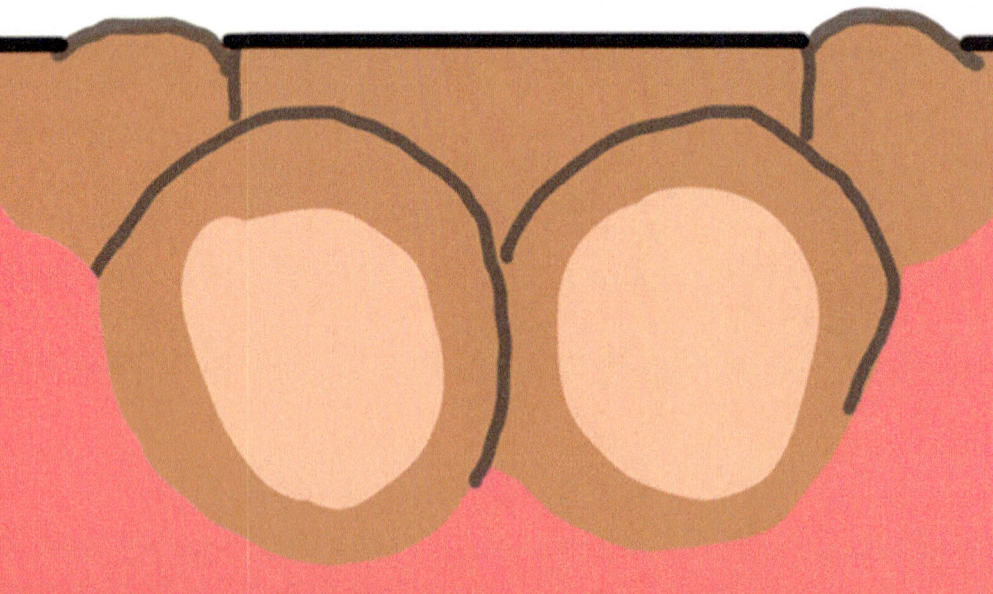

Meet the Reader with Steven!

In our new Meet the Reader series, you'll meet the readers behind KidsRead2Kids! First up is Steven, reader of the beloved classic, Peter Pan.

By Alana Blumenstein

Hi everyone! It's Alana from KidsRead2Kids. Recently, I got the chance to talk to our good friend, Steven, who is the reader of Peter Pan. We thought it'd be special to share our conversation with you!

Alana: Hi Steven! Thanks so much for joining us on our first Meet the Reader.

Steven: Hi, I'm so happy to be here and to be a part of this program. Today, I want to talk to you a little bit about myself and my love for reading.

A: Tell us about yourself!

S: My name is Steven, I'm 20 years old. I'm a nursing student, and I absolutely love it. I'm very excited to finally be in the field. I started reading when I was extremely young.

I have three siblings, and my mom thought that it was extremely important that all of us learn how to read when we were very little. And it has been a love of mine ever since.

Peter Pan: Chapter One

Scan to Watch

Read Me!

A: What were your favorite books growing up? What made them so special?

S: I have so many books from different areas of my life that really impacted me, including The Very Hungry Caterpillar by Eric Carl, The Giver by Lois Lowry, and the Divergent Series by Veronica Roth.

All the Places You'll Go by Dr. Seuss: When my mother was pregnant with my younger sibling … I read in the womb to him. I thought that it was so **imaginative** and so fun and so creative.

The Hunger Games by Suzanne Collins: I've read it probably five or six times, and I would read it again easily. I just remember being so inspired by the characters and how **fearless** they were.

I took that aspect and I actually applied it to my character in real life. I feel like those are the series that made the largest and most visible impact on my character.

A: What do you love about reading?

S: In first grade, I would pick up a book in class when it was free reading time, and I didn't even feel like I was there anymore. I loved the ability to **transport** myself into another world and to just be somewhere else and be **immersed** in another character's life.

"What I love most about reading is that it allows you to kind of get away, even if you're just at home or even if you're at school."

A: Did you have a favorite subject in school? Why?

S: Psychology and English. What I loved most about English was creative writing. That really allowed me to **unleash** my creativity and to put my own spin on whatever I was doing. I really liked that it was me, and it had my own **flair**, as opposed to just one book that everybody was reading.

A: Here at KidsRead2Kids, we believe our biggest struggles can also be our greatest strengths (or our real-life superpower!). What is YOUR superpower?

S: I used to struggle so much in middle school and most of my high school career with **determination** and focus and work ethic. It wasn't that I wasn't capable of learning the material, it's that I wasn't sitting down and dedicating myself. I was kind of trying to blow things off.

"Now I would say that's definitely my superpower. At a certain point, I just really wanted to be excellent at everything that I put my name on. If I was committed to a project, where I had a test coming up, and I had to sign my name at the top, I really wanted it to be 100%."

A: What, or who is your biggest inspiration? Why?

S: It's kind of corny, but I honestly would say that my inspiration in life as a person are my parents.

I was blessed with an incredible set of parents. They raised all four of their kids with such grace, and they were very loving people and very **adaptive**. I threw my parents many **curve-balls** growing up, and they love me **regardless**.

And outside of that, they are incredibly **diligent** workers. They love giving 100% and really going over the top and going that extra mile. So, I think that they are probably my biggest inspiration.

A: Did you have a role model growing up?

S: I know this sounds crazy. One of my huge role models is Beyoncé for that exact same reason. I think that she is an incredible artist and she has such an attention to detail. She just **dedicated** herself: no matter what it is, whether it's a single performance or an album or project, you will always see her giving 100% and going over the top and I really love that.

A: If you could change anything about the world, what would you change? Why?

S: I would certainly change how much **compassion** and **empathy** people have. I think that sometimes we forget to put ourselves in the shoes of others before we respond.

A: What advice would you give to the kids who look up to you?

S: That's crazy to think that there's a child that looks up to me, somewhere out there. To any child who's struggling to read, first of all, try to shift your **perspective** on reading.

Growing up, sometimes I would be assigned a book to read, and just because I was assigned the book, I automatically didn't want to read it because I looked at it as a task. I think that it's important to shift your perspective and look at it as something fun.

Find your **genre** of books that you will fall in love with. There's a book out there for absolutely everybody. Whether you love thrillers or action books, horror books, fantasy books, you should really go to your library.

Ask your librarian and say, 'I love these TV shows, or I love these genres. This really **intrigues** me; do you have any books that you would recommend for me?'

"Don't get discouraged. If the book seems lengthy, or there are words that you don't know, the only way that you will learn is to continuously expose yourself to them and keep reading. Just keep going and do your best to fall in love with the books that connect with you."

All the world is made of

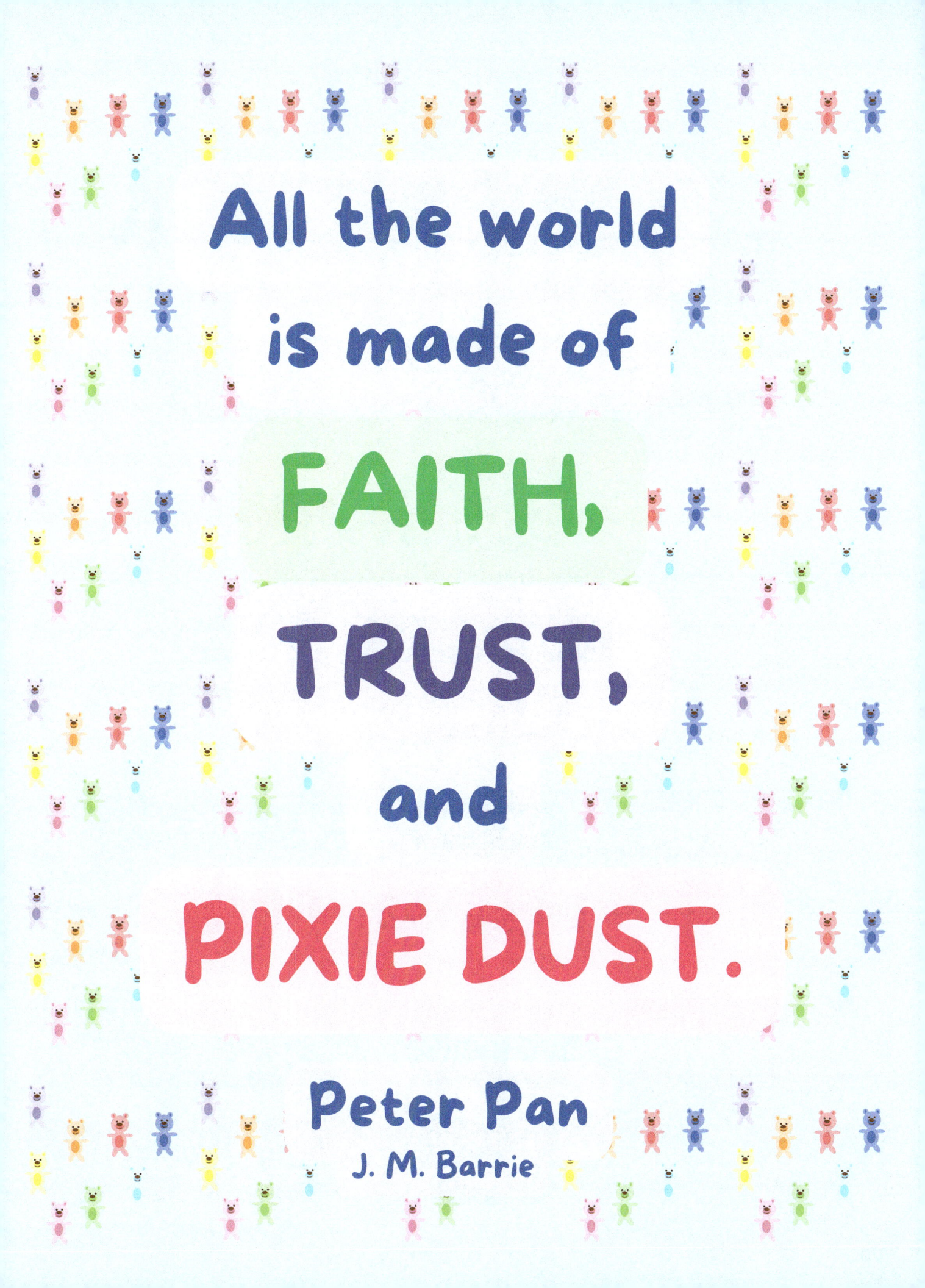

FAITH,

TRUST,

and

PIXIE DUST.

Peter Pan

J. M. Barrie

Which Peter Pan Character Are YOU?

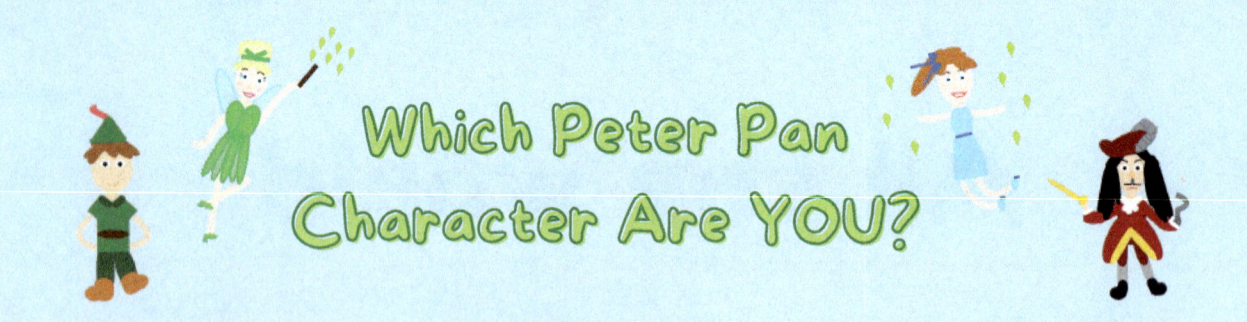

Choose two words to describe yourself:

- A) Fearless and loyal
- B) Mischievous and silly
- C) Caring and sweet
- D) Ambitious and strongwilled

Pick an activity.

- A) Swordfighting
- B) Flying
- C) Cooking
- D) Sailing

Who are you in a group?

- A) Leader
- B) Troublemaker
- C) Caretaker
- D) Lone Wolf

What is your fatal flaw?

- A) Stubborn and cocky
- B) Rely on attention from others
- C) Easily jealous
- D) Short tempered and fearful

If you have mostly...

A) You're Peter Pan! Like Peter, you are a fearless and loyal leader with a passion for adventure. Sometimes, you can be a little stubborn and cocky, but it's only because you care!

B) You're Tinkerbell! Like Tink, you are a mischievous and silly troublemaker with a big heart. You love deeply, and rely perhaps a bit too much on attention from others.

C) You're Wendy! Like Wendy, you are a thoughtful and kind caretaker, with a passion for helping others. Be careful you don't forget to take care of yourself, too!

D) You're Captain Hook! Like Hook, you are an ambitious and strong willed lone wolf with a dream to see the world. Try not to let your fear and short temper get the best of you!

Readers Around the Globe: It's Aarav!

In Meet the Reader (Kid Edition), you'll meet readers from around the world! First up is Aarav from Singapore.

By KidsRead2Kids Team

Hi Aarav! Thanks so much for joining us on our first Meet the Reader (Kid Edition!).

1. Where are you from? I was born in India but I have been in **Singapore** for over 5 years now.

2. Tell us about yourself! I am 7 years old. I am in Grade 2 and I just love to read. I along with my mother have read over 160 stories, live on Facebook, through our Facebook page bubsRus.

I also got an **opportunity** to read a story for the National Library Board of Singapore. Very recently, I presented a story at the FM Radio station - Radio Chutney. Playing with Beyblades and reading books makes me super happy.

3. What are your favorite books and why? Geronimo Stilton and Dogman series are my favorites because they are super funny.

4. What do you love about reading? I love the mystery in stories and the adventurous journey of different characters. Books open my mind to so many new things and it brings me to all these different places through my imagination, without actually visiting them.

5. Where is your favorite reading spot and why? I can read anywhere: at school, at the library, on the bus, even at my friend's birthday party!! But the most favorite spot would be the cozy corner in my room.

6. What were your biggest struggles in school, and how did you overcome them? I was not very good at Arts at school, but my mother made me practice it during the lock-down period. *DrawTogether with WendyMac* on YouTube has helped me become better. Also, I had a hard time accepting **defeat** at any games I played with my friends, but slowly I am learning to smile in the face of defeat :)

7. Here at KidsRead2Kids, we believe our biggest struggles can also be our greatest strengths (or our real-life superpower!). What is YOUR superpower? My mother tells me that my smile is my superpower. I also **forgive** very quickly, I hope it counts as a superpower :)

8. If you could change anything about the world, what would you change? Why? I would like Mother Earth to have more plants and plenty of water. I don't like water **pollution**; I hope people will stop throwing garbage in the water bodies.

9. What advice would you give to a kid struggling to read?

"I would tell them to not give up. They can start by reading easy books with lots of pictures and also listen to stories. Gradually, they can pick the harder books. There are so many books out there, pick one according to your interests and then you will fall in love with the world of books."

10 Questions with MANIAC Star Aaralyn Anderson

Since she was a baby, Aaralyn Anderson was destined to act. Today, at just 12-years-old, she's co-starred with Emma Stone and Jonah Hill in MANIAC, and will soon be featured in Full Circle on HBO Max.

1. How did you get started as an actress? What inspired you to pursue acting full-time? It wasn't until I was age 2 that I started acting. My first commercial was for Nickelodeon. As soon as the director called "ACTION," they could see a flip switch and I was on. From then on acting became my thing.

2. How do you memorize your lines? Being dyslexic reading didn't come easy so my mom would read the lines and I would repeat over and over again until I memorized them.

3. You costarred with Emma Stone and Jonah Hill on MANIAC. Any fun stories from set? MANIAC was an amazing experience. We go to the Table Read and my mom is handed paperwork. On the paper it says, Confirmed Cast, then lists Jonah Hill, Emma Stone, Julia Garner, then ... AARALYN ANDERSON. My mom almost passed out. We had no idea what I had booked walking into the table read. What was an audition for a 1-line costar role ended up being a principal cast role!

The craziest part was I met Emma about 8 months prior to this when both of us were making an appearance on Good Morning America. She remembered me!

4. As a dyslexic student, what is it like being home schooled? How do you balance your homework with the demands of a film career? I have always been dyslexic and home-schooled. I do like that I can focus at my own pace. In the last year I have learned two new languages. I have also learned to code. Things I never thought I would be able to do when I was younger. Being home-schooled allows me to not feel the stress that can sometimes make dyslexia worse.

MANIAC cast on the red carpet.

Anderson with Oscar-winning actress Emma Stone.

5. What advice would you give to someone interested in being an actor? Don't take rejection personally. There will be waaaaaaaaaay more No's than there are Yes's. But the No's are just as important as the Yes's. Sounds funny right? But it's true. You may not get a role that you think is made for you for a reason. A reason that might not have anything to do with you. You just never know. Best advice is to do the audition the best you can, send it and forget it. Trust the process.

Stay strong. Life may be rough at times but don't let it beat you down. Don't worry about what other people have to say about you. And like my mom says, "if it was easy, everyone would do it."

Readers Around the Globe: It's Karter!

In Meet the Reader (Kid Edition), you'll meet readers from around the world! Next up is Karter from Detroit, Michigan.

By KidsRead2Kids Team

Hi Karter! Welcome to the Kids Corner.

1. Tell us about yourself! I am the CEO and founder of Popcorn and Books. I created my business to help fight the literacy problem that some kids face. My goal is to show kids that reading can be fun and to be there for them if they need someone to read with, because just reading to kids could help improve their reading skills.

2. What are your favorite books and why?

My favorite book is from the Geronimo Stilton series because he is a very brainy rodent and has very funny stories. I love the way his books are played out and illustrated.

3. What do you love about reading? I love that reading can take you anywhere and you can meet all kinds of people and learn different stories - real or not.

4. Where is your favorite reading spot and why? Reading is like going to the movies but in your head without the screen so I love sitting on my Big Joe seat in my room with a big bowl of popcorn.

5. Here at KidsRead2Kids, we believe our biggest struggles can also be our greatest strengths (or our real-life superpower!). What is YOUR superpower? My superpower is doing book reviews and writing them myself!

6. If you could change anything about the world, what would you change? Why? If I could change the world I would encourage kids to read more and enjoy reading because I just want to see kids happy.

7. What advice would you give to a kid struggling to read?

"If you are struggling with reading listen to audio-books or watch people read on YouTube. This way you can enjoy many different stories and become interested in reading which would make practicing a lot less painful."

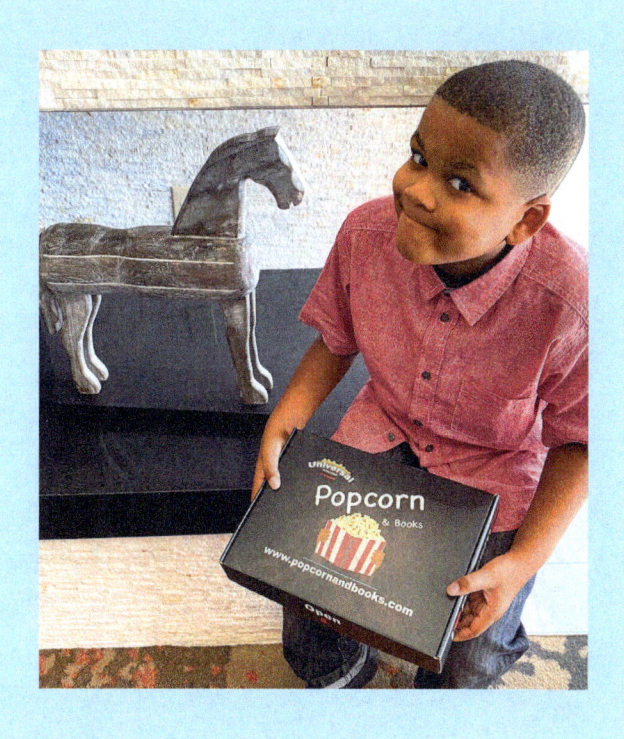

Now, a few quick favorites!

Favorite author: Geronimo Stilton

Favorite writing style: Action

Hobbies: reading on my Facebook page, Popcorn and Books!

Want to be featured next? Let us know at info@kidsread2kids.com.

Brynjar Karl Broke a World Record with Nothing But LEGOs

Brynjar Karl, 17, is best known for building the largest LEGO Titanic worldwide. But he was just ten at the time, crediting his child-like thinking and autistic mind.

By Alana Blumenstein

When Brynjar Karl broke the world record for building the largest LEGO Titanic, he had no idea his life would change. Born in Reykjavik, Iceland, Brynjar was just ten when he built the 26-foot-long replica — and his story went viral.

At 17, he is charming, expressive, and kind, with a big heart and a mission to help others. **But his greatest gift? His autism.**

"I had a rough childhood, but a big dream," says Brynjar on a Zoom with KidsRead2Kids. "I wanted to do something special and it became much bigger than I expected."

The project required over 56,000 LEGO bricks, 700 hours, and eleven, long months. Today, his work is featured at the Titanic Museum in Pigeon Forge, Tennessee, where it has been seen by over two million visitors.

Brynjar credits his child-like thinking for his success. "When you're a child, you … want to think big," he says. "When you're an adult, or even like, at my age, you think, 'It's not gonna work.'"

Brynjar's big dream soon went viral — all thanks to a Kickstarter campaign. His video, which kindly asked the public if they could help him "accumulate 56 thousand Lego cubes," received over 67K views on YouTube. Eleven months later, Brynjar was featured on Discovery Science, CBS News, and other major channels.

Today, Brynjar is proudest of his journey with autism. Since the project, he says his social skills have greatly improved, allowing him to engage in conversations. "I can keep a conversation going now," he explains. "But when I was young, I couldn't even bother doing things like this."

Admiral Brynjar reporting for duty!

His mother, Bjarney Ludviksdottir, was well familiar with his behavior. "He wasn't able to attract kids," she explains. "He didn't know how to make that connection." Bjarney adds that, in the past, her son sometimes used strange words and didn't know how to make friends.

Brynjar was five years old when he was first diagnosed, but he wasn't given the news until much later. What he didn't see was the team his mother had gathered behind him. "In Iceland, we are not so much ahead like you in these things," Bjarney says. "I'm proud of the people that were supporting him."

Brynjar and Bjarney.

Karl with his record-breaking LEGO Titanic; The Titanic Museum in Pigeon Forge, TN.

Alongside his teachers, Bjarney developed a plan for her son. Brynjar's teachers worked hard to ensure he had a positive experience. Their ethic and kindness quickly made an impact on Brynjar's education and life.

When Brynjar was around nine or ten, his diagnosis was explained.

"They told me that I was a bit different," he says. But he didn't feel different at all, adding that he took the news in stride. "That's not gonna change me because I'm still me," Brynjar says. "That doesn't make me any worse in any sense."

Soon after, Brynjar set to build the largest LEGO Titanic, and the blocks fell into place. "He was always training his communication skills," Bjarney says, adding that visitors often came to his building site. "When he got the opportunity to talk about his interest, then he could communicate."

Bjarney believes passion was the key to her son's success. "It doesn't matter if it's autism, ADHD, dyslexia," she says. "When they're allowed to develop through their interest, something sparks.

Brynjar's Advice to Kids With a Dream: Go for It!

Today, their mission is far from over. Brynjar's documentary, How the Titantic Became My Lifeboat, premiered in April 2021. A producer and director, Bjarney has four years of experience with documentaries. One day, it occurred to her that Brynjar's story needed to be shared with the world.

"I'm the mother always with the camera, always recording," she laughs. "I found myself having loads of material on my desk, and I thought to myself, why not … make a documentary out of it?"

Brynjar explains they wanted to be an example for others. "People usually think of autism like it's a bad thing," he says.

In sharing his journey, **Brynjar strives to give hope and to educate others** on what it's like to be autistic. "We want to give that story to everyone to make everyone understand how I felt, but … **there's a big change if you just let them dream big."**

On that note, **Bjarney encourages parents to support their child's dreams.** When a child comes up with a crazy idea, it's very easy to say, "let's talk later and forget about it," she says. But she urges parents to think again.

"My message to parents is stop and think and see if you can maybe find a way to help the kid get there on his own," she says. "That's what we did. We were … behind him, he was leading the way."

81

The Karl Family.

Still, Brynjar's own big dreams revolve around the sea. He is currently working at a whale washing company. "I think the sea life is actually pretty amazing," he says. "When I'm on, it's just like, you're gliding."

His dreams don't end there. He even hopes to run his own ship one day. "I want to become a captain," Brynjar says. "That's my next target."

He's aware that it's a big ambition, he says. But Brynjar isn't worried. On the contrary, he believes in himself and his abilities — and the world should too. "I think I can absolutely do it," he tells us.

His message to kids is the same. "You shouldn't be scared for it because it's a dream," he says. "I say go for it."

Even if it means breaking a world record.

Brynjar (center) speaking at a school.

We can change the world and make it a better place.

It is in our hands to make a difference.

Nelson Mandela

UN Young Leader Siena Castellon Celebrates Neurodiversity

Siena Castellon wants to celebrate our differences. Through her platform Quantum Leap Mentoring, she is changing the narrative on learning challenges.

By Alana Blumenstein

18-year-old Siena Castellon is proud to be autistic. The UN Young Leader talks openly about her experiences with dyslexia, dyspraxia, ADHD and anxiety, to help others celebrate what makes them different. **Through her platform Quantum Leap Mentoring, Castellon aims to change the narrative on neurodiversity.**

At just 13-years-old, Castellon began to see a problem in her local community in London. Those around her seemed to only focus on the negative aspects of learning differences.

Every single time I was told what I couldn't do," Castellon says of her diagnosis. "I was never told the positives."

She hoped to provide empowering support and mentorship for kids like her. "I found that there was a real lack of resources for children with learning differences," she says. While there was access to information for teachers and parents, Castellon says the same wasn't true for kids.

At the time, she wished to find tips for the little things, such as paying attention with ADHD or acing a spelling test with dyslexia.

Frustrated, Castellon spent hours searching for advice to no avail, finding sprinkles here and there. One day, she had an epiphany. She realized there was a need for a central hub, which gathered all of the information in one place. **Castellon decided she would build it herself, and QL Mentoring was born.**

Castellon shares her story to show others that they are not alone, no matter their struggle. On QL Mentoring, you can find information on a range of learning challenges as well as Castellon's personal advice. She provides tips on many topics, including bullying, which she says is common for kids with autism.

In childhood, Castellon recalls her own experience of being called stupid and lazy.

> **"When I was younger, and I was being bullied, I would take what I would hear as the truth,"** Castellon says, adding that **the bullying negatively affected her self-esteem.**

Though she initially felt defeated, she learned to brush off hateful comments.

> "I would tell my parents afterwards, and we would just laugh about it," she remembers.

Castellon explains that when it comes to bullies, the best thing to do is reject their view entirely.

Soon after launching QL Mentoring, Castellon began receiving messages from kids like her. "People started to contact me and share their stories," she says. Many of them had one thing in common: they felt limited by the outside world.

85

"They're trying to be inspired by the difference, but the wider community isn't allowing them to do that," Castellon says.

She believes many people have their own narratives of what it means to have a learning difference, whether it's autism or dyslexia. Unfortunately, misconceptions like these are everywhere, including our school systems.

Castellon explains that this limiting perspective can make neurodiverse students feel less than their classmates and incapable of the same achievements. "You're not made to feel empowered," Castellon says — something she strives to change.

This misconception drove her to start Neurodiversity Celebration Week, a movement she hopes to spread to schools worldwide. The program, which encourages schools to recognize and celebrate neurodiverse students, reached over half a million students and 720 schools in its first year.

"They got to hear all the positives of learning differences," Castellon says. This act of celebration is just one way Castellon aims to change the narrative. Her book, which was a game-changer for autistic girls, is another.

In The Spectrum Girl's Survival Guide: How to Grow Up Awesome and Autistic, Castellon shares personal tips on friendships, body image, bullying, and more. "I started thinking about this disconnect in the way girls present and the way boys present," she says, adding that she could only find advice written by men.

"While I was writing it, I realized that it was going to be the first book written for autistic girls by an autistic girl." From the illustrator to the author to the foreword, Castellon ensured that her team was made up entirely of autistic women.

SIENA CASTELLON

YOUNG LEADERS
SUSTAINABLE DEVELOPMENT GOALS

Castellon's advocacy led her to be nominated to the United Nations Young Leaders Class of 2020. When she heard the news of her acceptance, she couldn't believe it. "I was just so happy," she says. "I felt like I was going to be able to make a difference in the community and get a message out there that's important and that needs to be heard."

Though neurodiversity attracts bullies, Castellon has gained strength from her experiences. "When I was younger ... I was very into people-pleasing," she says, adding that she didn't want to be perceived as difficult. **Today, Castellon has learned to stand up for herself, and she encourages others to do the same.**

"Make a distinction between what's helpful and what's harmful," she advises. "Don't take criticism from people you wouldn't take advice from."

To become a changemaker, Castellon suggests utilizing social media and sharing your own stories. She explains that her advocacy is stronger because she's able to connect with her audience on a deeper level. "Because I was able to relate to the people that I was talking to ... there was a personal element to my advocacy," she says.

Being neurodiverse can be difficult, she admits, but Castellon happily celebrates her differences.

"I'm lucky that I'm autistic, dyslexic, dyspraxic, and have ADHD," she shares. Thanks to her neurodiversity, Castellon is an excellent problem solver, is naturally creative, and sees the world through a unique lens.

From acing a spelling test with dyslexia to focusing with ADHD to managing anxiety, Castellon has conquered nearly every problem. Looking back at her life, she feels nothing but gratitude for her journey.

How wonderful it is that nobody need wait

A SINGLE MOMENT

before starting to

IMPROVE THE WORLD.

Anne Frank

BIG IDEAS
Lessons From Our Mentors...

1. Steven
Don't get discouraged. Keep trying: find the books and genres that excite you.

2. Aarav
Learn to accept defeat with grace. There is power in forgiveness!

3. Aaralyn
Don't take rejection personally. Stay strong, keep trying, and trust the process.

4. Karter
Reading is FUN! If you are struggling, try listening to an audiobook.

5. Brynjar
Find a passion and believe in your dreams. You can do ANYTHING!

6. Siena
Stay true to yourself, celebrate your differences, and stand up for others like you.

... Books are MAGICAL!

"If there is a

book

that you want to

read,

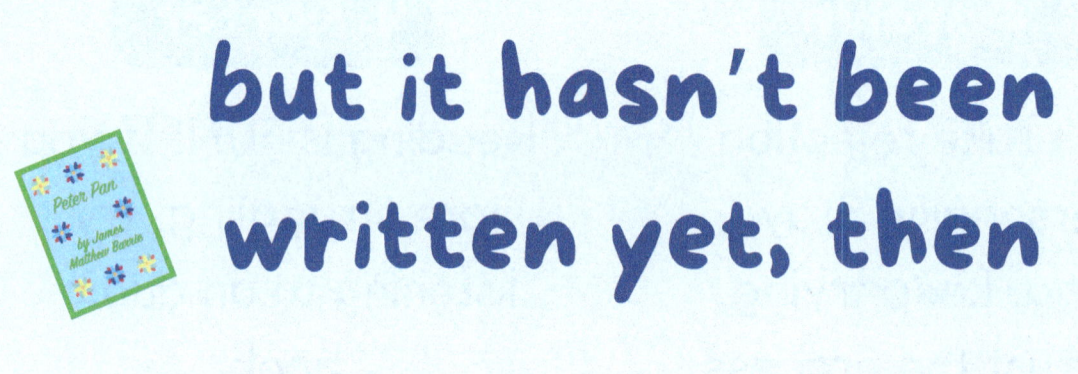

but it hasn't been

written yet, then

YOU must write it."

- Toni Morrison

YOUR TURN!

1. What's YOUR favorite book and why?

2. Name three things you love about reading.

3. Choose FIVE vocab words from our collection. (See page 213)

4. Which mentor did you relate to the most? What do you admire about them?

5. Name three lessons you've learned from their stories.

6. What's YOUR real-life superpower?

7. What advice would you give to someone like you?

8. What would you change about the world and why?

9. Name three ways you can make a difference in your daily life. (Ex: be a good friend, volunteer, say thank you, etc.)

It's not what the
world holds for you,

it's what you
bring to it.

Anne of Green Gables

L.M. Montgomery

Our Favorite Things

Ready, Set, STEM!

Making Play Dough!

Scan to Watch

Make Your Own Volcano!

Ingredients:
Playdough (any color), 1-ounce vinegar, 1-ounce baking soda, Film canister, Food coloring, Dish soap, 1 pan with lid (keep your space clean)

Instructions:

1. Pour the baking soda into the film canister
2. Place the playdough on the pan
3. Mold it into the shape of a volcano
4. Make a deep hole in the center
5. Place your film canister inside
6. Add a drop or 2 of dish soap to your vinegar.
7. Add food coloring!
8. Now pour the vinegar mix into the film canister and watch your volcano erupt!

Our Favorite School Treat: Protein Bites

Protein Bites are the perfect piece of brain food to start the day. Here's a recipe we know you'll love.

One of our favorite treats to make is our Protein Bites. We found the recipe a few years back (thanks Trader Joes!) and have been in love ever since.

Though we modify the original to suit our allergies (gluten-free, dairy-free), the taste is just as good. These Protein Bites are small but full of nutrients.

For this reason, they are one of our favorite school snacks. We know being a student comes with the dread of early mornings (and the sleepiness, too!).

That's why Protein Bites are the perfect piece of brain food to start the day. They fill our bodies with the energy we need to succeed.

Ingredients

Dry

- 1 cup rolled oats (we love to use Trader Joes gluten-free rolled oats)
- ½ cup chocolate chips (dairy-free, milk, dark, semi-sweet, etc.)
- ½ cup ground flaxseed meal (can substitute ground chai or half chai/half flaxseed)

Wet

- ½ cup crunchy peanut butter (can substitute almond butter or sun butter)
- ⅓ cup honey (can substitute maple syrup)
- 1 teaspoon vanilla

Instructions

Combine all ingredients together in a bowl. Roll into one-inch balls, either with your hands or a one-inch cookie scoop. We like to use a cookie scoop for consistency.

Line a freezer-safe container with a wax paper square. Fill the bottom with your finished protein bites.

When the layer is full, top it with wax paper and continue onto the next row. Once complete, line the top with wax paper and put it on the cover.

Freeze for at least an hour. We like to let them set overnight. In the morning, they're ready to eat! Let each bite thaw for 10 minutes before eating.

Our Favorite Breakfasts

(Enjoy these simple meals on-the-go or at home!)

Strawberry Banana Smoothie

In a blender, add:
1 banana, 1/2 pint strawberries, 2 peeled oranges, 1 oz honey, 2 cups ice
Blend, serve & enjoy!

Peanut Butter Smoothie

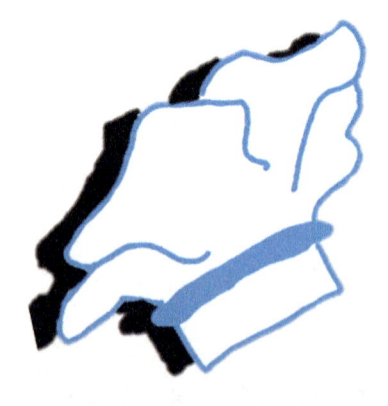

In a blender, add:
1 banana, 3/4 cup soy milk, 1/4 cup peanut butter, one scoop vanilla protein powder, honey to taste, 1 cup ice
Blend, serve & enjoy!

Egg Bites

Ingredients:
6 scrambled eggs, 1 cup cottage cheese, 1/2 cup shredded cheese, 1/2 cup chopped mushrooms, 1/2 cup chopped onion, 1 cup spinach

Instructions:
1. Blend eggs and cottage cheese in blender.
2. Saute vegetables.
3. Mix together in bowl.
4. Pour evenly in muffin tin.
5. Bake at 350 degrees for 20 minutes.

Serves 12. Enjoy!

Avocado Toast

Instructions:
1. Toast bread.
2. Spread ricotta cheese.
3. Top with mashed avocado.
4. Add arugula and tomato.
5. Drizzle with honey.
6. Optional: Serve with fried egg on top.

Ingredients:
1 piece sprouted or wheat bread, 1/4 cup ricotta cheese, 1/2 of peeled or mashed avocado, 1/8 tsp Nature's Seasons, arugula, chopped tomato, honey, fried egg

Our Favorite Apps

Navigating life with a learning disability can be challenging. It's easy to feel lost or overwhelmed. So, here are the tools that we use to survive!

"Speechify is an app I use all the time! It reads out my textbooks to me in almost any form. For me, it can be really hard and intimidating to read. Having an app like Speechify makes life so much easier!"

Jacob: Speechify

"Discord is definitely my favorite app. I use it to study and collaborate on projects with friends! Discord even lets you set your study goals and sends reminders to keep you motivated. It's really cool!"

Reuben: Discord

"Otter is a lifesaver with interviews for the magazine. It records and transcribes everything for me, which saves so much time and effort. You can even use it to record your school lectures!"

Alana: Otter

"I love listening to stories on Audible. Reading on paper has always been hard for me. Audible gives me the chance to have any book read to me at my own pace. It's really fun!"

Carol: Audible

"Supernotes keeps all of my notes, lists, and random thoughts together in a fully-searchable space! I have trouble keeping all of my thoughts together, and Supernotes helps me see through the chaos."

Benjamin: Supernotes

Other Tools We Love:

Grammarly - don't be afraid to get your grammar checked!

OneNote - keep all your documents in one place!

Bookshare - a free digital library, w/ proof of a learning disability

Any.do - a digital planner to use on the go!

Duolingo - an interactive way to learn languages

Understood.org - a lifelong guide for those who learn differently

kR2K presents...

KIDS IN THE CRAFTROOM

We Made Bear-Noculars   And You Can, Too!

MAKING YOUR BINOCULARS!

Scan to Watch

We Made Bear-Noculars, and You Can Too!

Our Bear-Noculars are super fun and so easy to make. Just follow these steps, and you'll be bear hunting in no time!

Materials:
2 toilet paper rolls, 1 paper clip, 1 sheet of cardstock paper, 1 piece of tape, 1 rubber band, 1 ribbon

Instructions:

1. Take the two toilet paper rolls and paper clip them together
2. Fold the paper in half hotdog style
3. Fold the ends of the paper in two inches
4. Set the rolls in the middle of the strip
5. Wrap the folded end around the rolls
6. Tightly wrap the other side on top
7. Tape it together
8. Flip it over, so the taped part is on the bottom
9. Stretch the rubber band over one of the rolls and have it rest in the middle, creasing the paper
10. Wrap the ribbon around the rubber band in the middle of the rolls and tie

We're Going on a Bear Hunt!

Hi. I'm Reuben.

I'm 17 years old, and one of the Co-Founders of KidsRead2Kids. I'm here to walk you through my favorite activity from a really exciting project called the KidsRead2Kids Book Club.

In September 2020, we founded KidsRead2Kids Book Club to take our mission of bringing joy and confidence to struggling learners one step further. We wanted to peer-mentors and resources into the hands of kids in need, especially during such a lonely and isolated time. In our pilot runs at our local schools and organizations, hundreds have had a blast with us!

Now, follow me through our first ever Bear Hunt scavenger hunt in December 2020, which we've since repeated with dozens of new friends!

In December 2020, we brought our Bear Hunt to life for the very first time in Downtown Birmingham Michigan to bring COVID-safe activity to families and help local businesses. It was a city-wide scavenger hunt where our brave Bear Finders tracked down our KidsRead2Kids Reading Bears!

To get ready to search, we read the book *We're Going on a Bear Hunt* by Michael Rosen. We train to interactively read, which means pausing to ask questions and making sure we're all engaging with the material!

Benjamin and Alana set up posters in Downtown Birmingham, MI.

After we finished reading and asking questions, we each learned to make our own Bear-Noculars! The Bear-Noculars activity is super easy, and a great way to prepare to become an official Bear Finder!

A future Bear Finder participates in the Bear Hunt!

So... do YOU have what it takes to become a Professional Bear Finder?

Email info@kidsread2kids.com to bring our Bear Hunt to you!

There is no friend as loyal as a book.

Ernest Hemingway

Your Turn!

What Kind of Reader Are You?

Take the Quiz to Find Your Genre

Pick a main character description.
- A. Hopeless romantic
- B. Brave adventurer
- C. Curious thinker
- D. Magical spellcaster

My protagonist dreams of...
- A. Meeting their soulmate
- B. Experiencing an epic journey
- C. Finding hidden clues
- D. Opening a portal to a new world

My protagonist...
- A. Has a secret crush
- B. Loves to travel
- C. Asks a lot of questions
- D. Possesses hidden powers

My book makes me feel...
- A. Dreamy and starry-eyed
- B. Ready to explore
- C. Like a true detective
- D. Like a wizard or superhero!

A. You got Romance!

You guessed it: romance stories are all about love. You're a fan of crushes, soulmates, deep friendships, and everything gooey and sweet! Here's some books to make your heart flutter!

Stargirl
by Jerry Spinelli

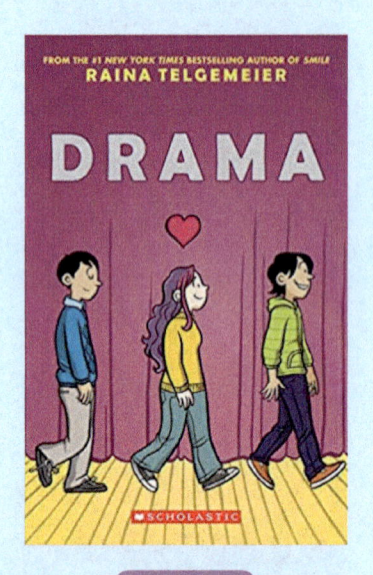

Drama
by Raina Telgmeier

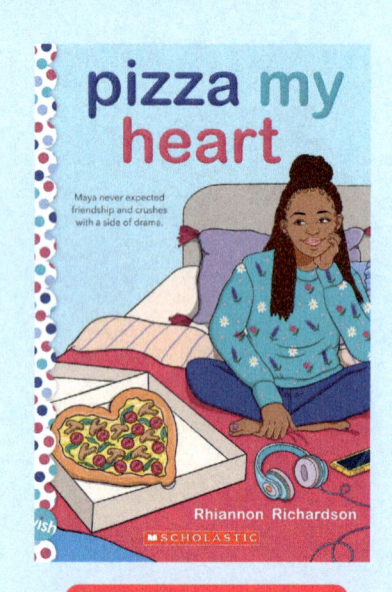

Pizza My Heart
by Rhiannon Richardson

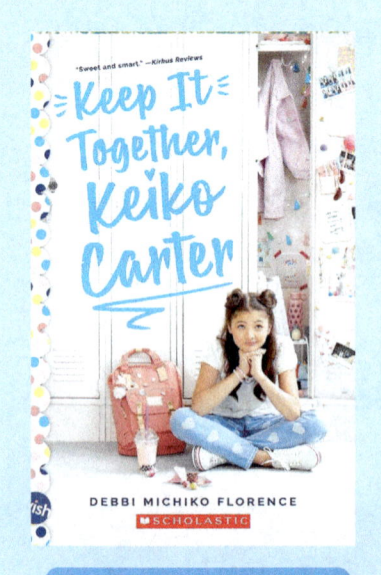

Keep It Together,
Keiko Carter
by Debbi Michiko Florence

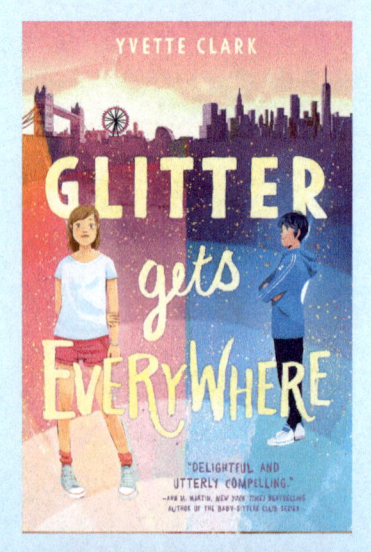

Glitter Gets Everywhere
by Yvette Clark

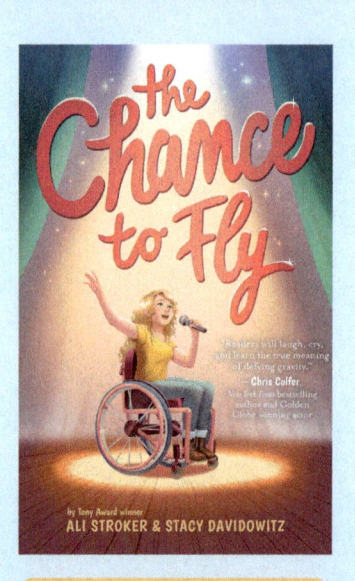

The Chance to Fly
by Ali Stroker &
Stacy Davidowitz

B. You got Action-Adventure!

You love exciting and dangerous stories with epic journeys. Your protagonist is on a mission and ready to face any obstacle they may encounter. Here are some action-packed books filled with adventure!

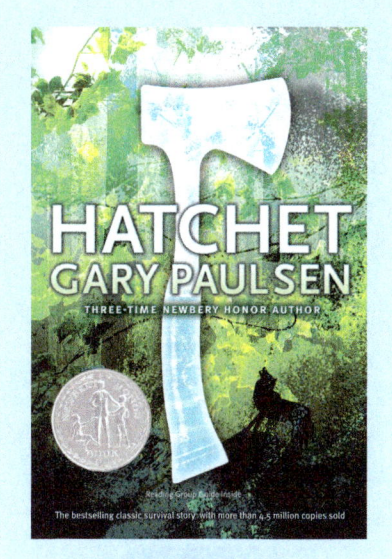

Hatchet
by Gary Paulsen

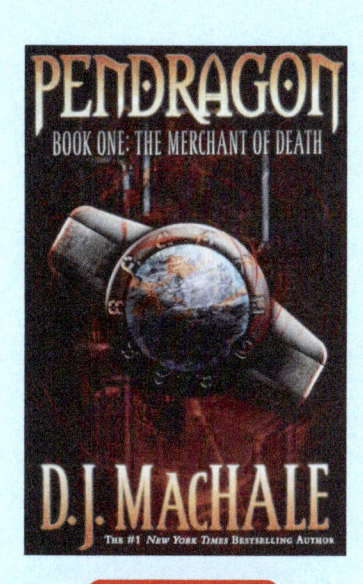

Pendragon
by D.J. MacHale

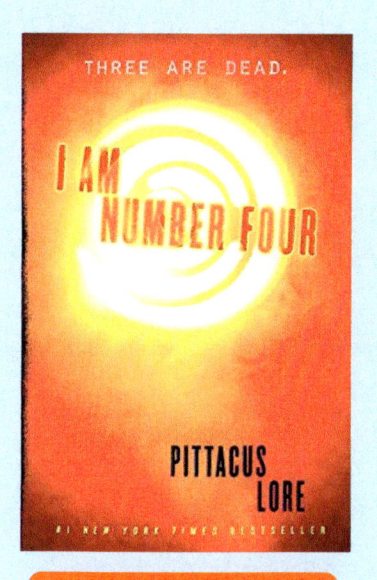

I Am Number Four
by Pittacus Lore

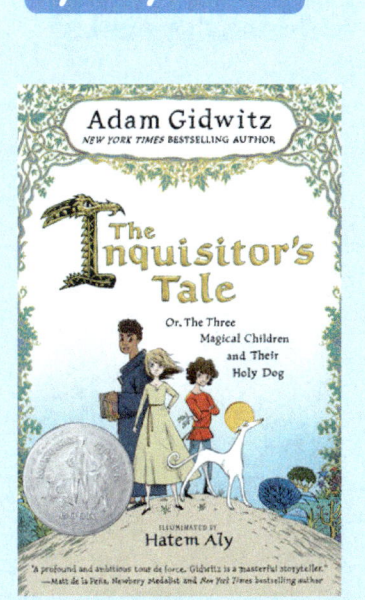

The Inquisitor's Tale
by Adam Gidwitz

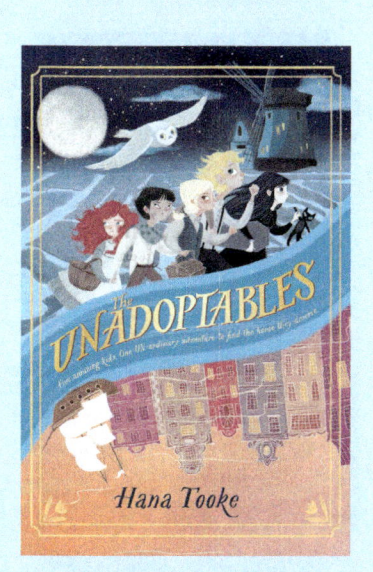

The Unadoptables
by Hana Tooke

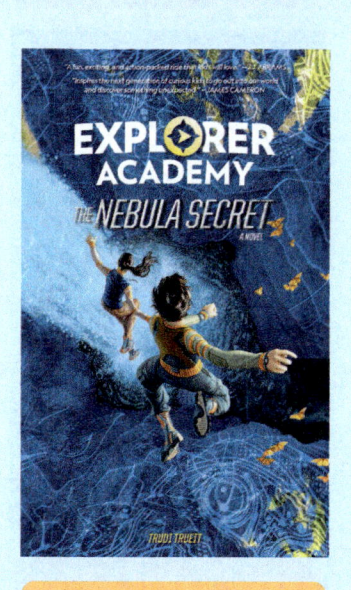

Explorer Academy
by Trudi Truiet

C. You got Mystery!

You love asking questions, finding clues, and solving mysteries. Your protagonist could be a detective, or even an onlooker who gets wrapped up in mysterious circumstances... Here are some books to die for!

The Mysterious Benedict Society by Trenton Lee Stewart

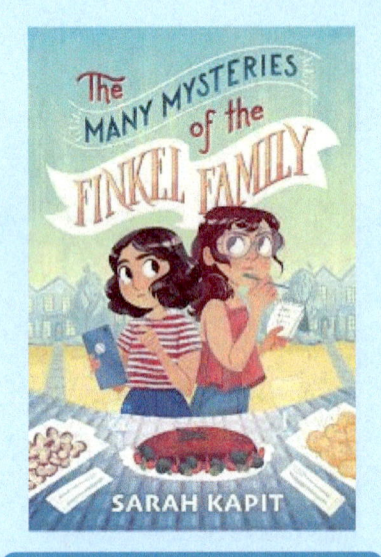

The Many Mysteries of the Finkel Family by Sarah Kapit

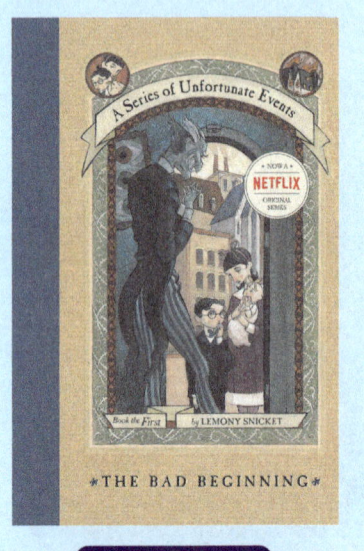

A Series of Unfortunate Events by Lemony Snicket

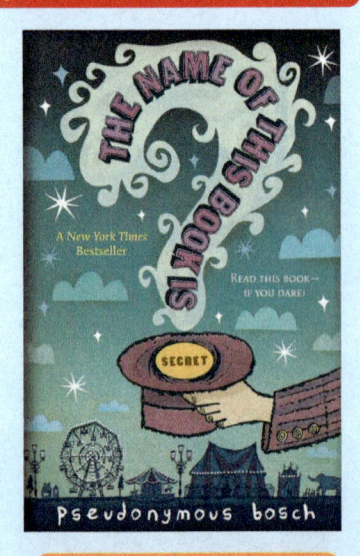

The Name of This Book is Secret by Pseudonymous Bosch

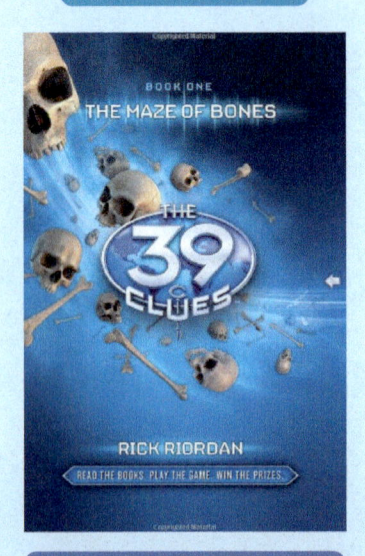

39 Clues: The Maze of Bones by Rick Riordan

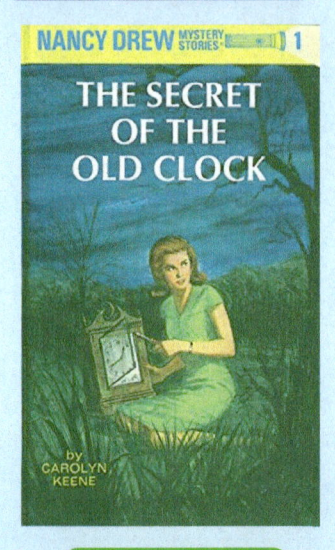

Nancy Drew by Carolyn Keene

D. You got Fantasy!

You love magical, fantastical stories that take you somewhere new. Your protagonist may have superpowers, hidden abilities, or a deadly secret. Here are some fantasy books that are out of this world!

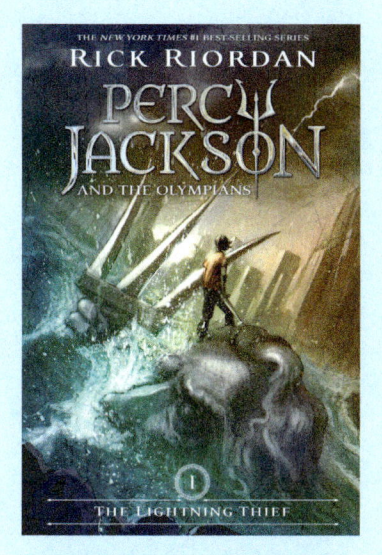

The Lightning Thief by Rick Riordan

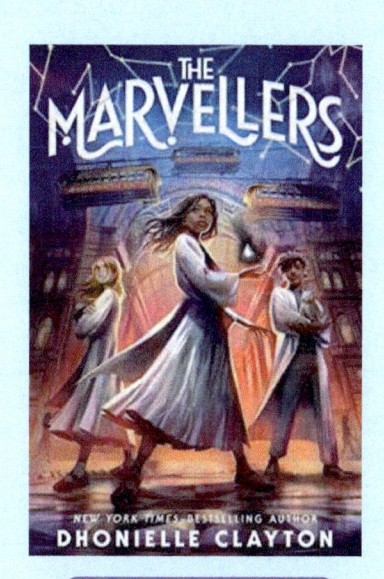

The Marvellers by Dhonielle Clayton

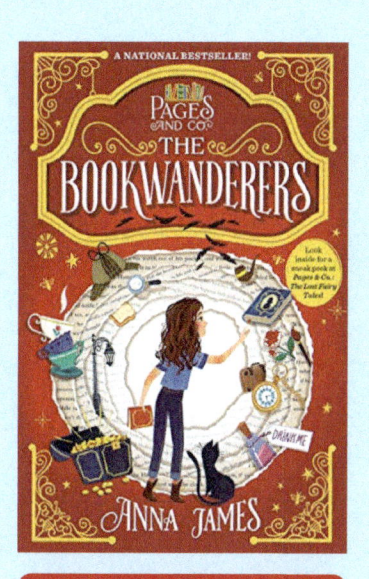

The Bookwanderers by Anna James

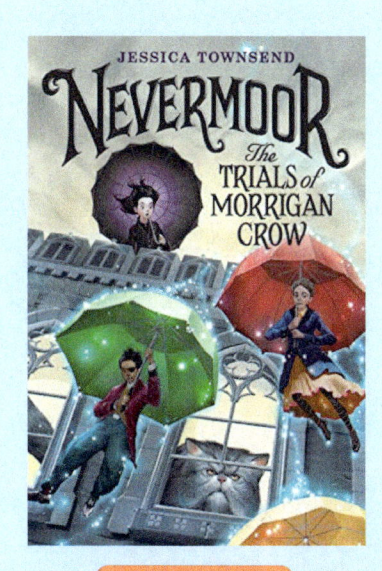

Nevermoor by Jessica Townsend

The School for Good and Evil by Soman Chainani

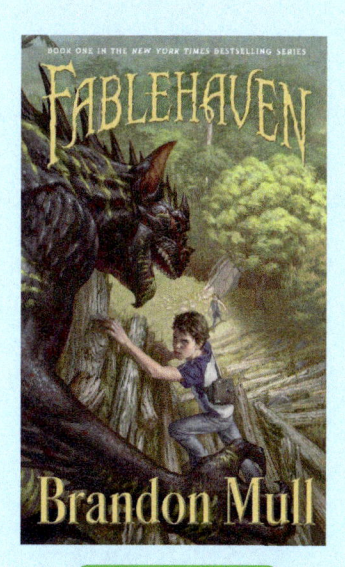

Fablehaven by Brandon Mull

My Favorite Book List

Find a book you like? Write it down here for safekeeping!

Send your book suggestions to us at info@kidsread2kids.com

Books are the mirrors of the soul.

Virginia Woolf

The Reading Nest:

Alana: The Winnie Years Series by Lauren Myracle

Meet Winnie. She's funny, daring, sensitive, and dramatic. Each book starts with a new birthday and every chapter covers another month in her life. Young girls will identify with the funny challenges and joys in Winnie's life.

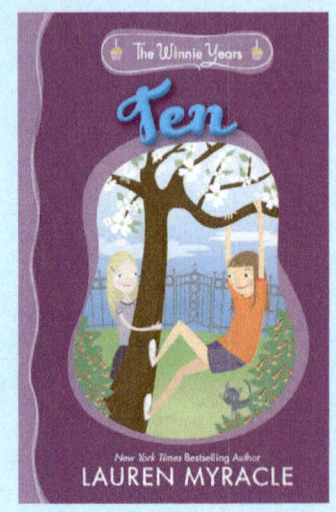

Jacob: A Wrinkle in Time by Madeleine L'Engle

The story of Meg Murry, who is transported on an adventure through time and space with her younger brother Charles Wallace and her friend Calvin O'Keefe to rescue her father, a gifted scientist, from the evil forces that hold him prisoner on another planet.

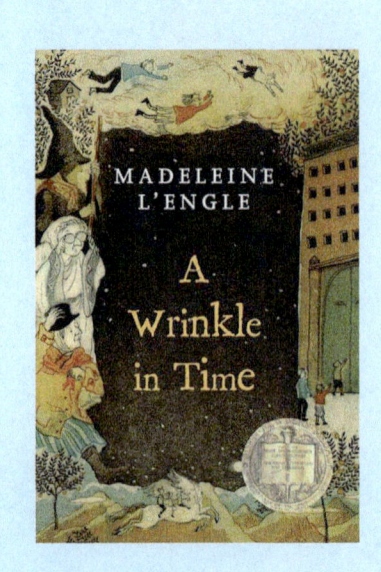

Our Favorite Books

Julia: Middle School: The Worst Years of My Life by Chris Tebbetts and James Patterson

Rafe has enough problems at home without throwing his first year of middle school into the mix. Luckily, he's got an ace plan for the best year ever: to break every rule in his school's oppressive Code of Conduct. But when Rafe's game starts to catch up with him, he'll have to decide if winning is all that matters, or if he's finally ready to face the rules, bullies, and truths he's been avoiding.

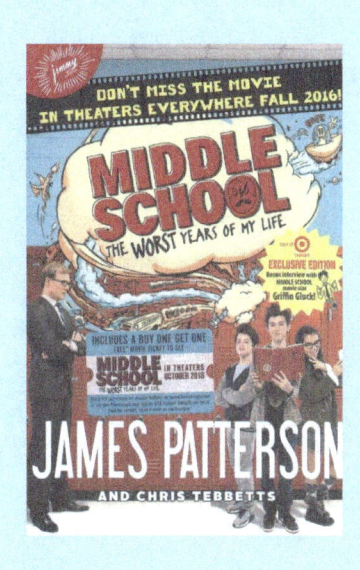

Reuben: Ms. Bixby's Last Day by John David Anderson

There are different kinds of teachers: the boring ones, the mean ones, and the ones who stopped trying long ago. Ms. Bixby is none of these. Topher, Brand, and Steve know this better than anyone. And so, when Ms. Bixby unexpectedly announces that she won't be able to finish the school year, they come up with a risky plan to give Ms. Bixby the last day she deserves.

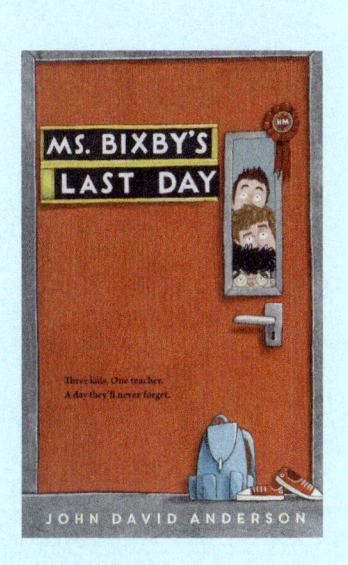

Librarian's Corner: Welcome Ashley!

In the Librarian's Corner, librarians share their favorite stories. Meet Ashley from West Marion Elementary School!

Book #1: Full of Beans by Jennifer Holm
Ages 8-12+, Grade Level 3-7

Grown-ups lie. That's one truth Beans knows for sure. He and his gang know how to spot a whopper a mile away. Not that Beans really minds; it's 1934, the middle of the Great Depression. With no jobs on the island, and no money anywhere, who can really blame the grown-ups for telling a few tales? Besides, Beans isn't anyone's fool. In fact, he has plans. Big plans. And the consequences might surprise even Beans himself.

Scan to Watch

Are you a librarian with a story to share?
Reach out to us at info@kidsread2kids.com.

From Our Teachers:

I'd Like To...
by Mrs. Hickerson
6th Grade Language Arts Teacher

I'd like to be a globe, so I could travel the world with just one spin.

I'd like to be an NFL football, traveling to all the stadiums across the country.

I'd like to be a well-worn suitcase, with scuffs, scrapes and dents which mirrors how life can be.

I'd like to be a passport, stamped with all the countries I only dream about traveling to, so dreams can become a reality.

I'd like to be a hiking boot to stomp across the forest, plains and prairie so I am able to explore the unknown.

I'd like to be a bird, so I can take in the world and its wonders from a different perspective and experience it to the fullest.

I'd like to just be...

Are you a teacher with a poem to share?
Reach out to us at info@kidsread2kids.com.

A poem begins in DELIGHT and ends in WISDOM.

Robert Frost

The Universe Poem

by Thomas Stapp

a middle schooler just like you!

While the subways and taxis loud as Harlem on a Friday, as loud as a jukebox on full bass, I see the platinum-colored cars drive down the Berlin Lane where, on the sides, nature flourishes, mountains with a wild gaze.

The iron and stone behemoth with a strong grasp. While an asteroid is going to crash.

The floods of love rush out, strong as a tsunami on the big city, the silver buildings have to flee, but there they stand like trees.

The people rush to the emerald hills. The aquamarine waves crash onto the lavender land.

The buttercups bloom, as serenity falls upon the land, a king's crown studded with opal and rubies and sapphires on the gold frame.

As the sound of a paradise far away enters the ears of the sad, lame, and poor, the rainbow of life shooting out from the diamond prism, the aurora of an eclipse with its amethyst gaze.

The iridescent neon of lights of passion, love, strength, happiness, and other feelings that live bottled-up inside of you.

That's the truth.

So live life to the fullest, be nice to others, and treat others the way you want to be treated.

Don't have a heart made of a glacier.

I dwell in POSSIBILITY.

Emily Dickinson

I can be...
by Alana Blumenstein

Last night I dreamed I was an artist. I drew and drew and drew until my hand began to cramp, and the pages were covered in color.

Last week I dreamed I was an inventor. I inspired new ideas and creations that no one had ever thought of before.

Last month I dreamed I was an actress. My smile lit up screens on your television. My tears pulled heartstrings across the globe.

Last year I dreamed I was an author. I wrote and wrote and wrote until my stories had comforted even the loneliest of souls.

I once dreamed I was an astronaut. I flew past the moon and touched the stars, blasting off, higher and higher, until my head landed softly on my pillow.

I woke up and I was me.

Me the artist. Me the inventor. Me the actress. Me the author. Me the astronaut.

Me the dreamer.

I can be it all.

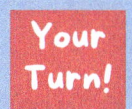

YOUR TURN!

Use the format above (or create your own). Write an "I Can Be" poem!

Last night I dreamed I was...

What Will YOU Be?

Circle the careers that inspire you!

Teacher: I want to help kids be the best they can be!

Coder: I want to make websites & apps!

Astronaut: I want to explore and discover!

Musician: I want to tell stories through music!

Artist: I want to draw, paint, CREATE!

Scientist: I love asking questions and solving problems

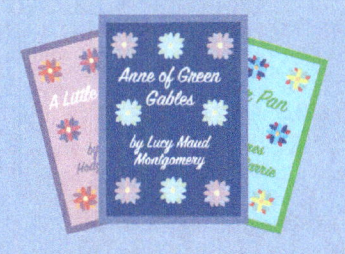

Author: I want to share my stories with the world!

Baker: I love making cookies, muffins, anything sweet!

Advocate: I want to make the world a better place

Stylist: I want to make people feel beautiful!

Mechanic: I'm handy and love to tinker!

Sailor: I want to be the captain of my own ship!

Farmer: I love nature and working with animals

Toymaker: I want to make play more fun!

Performer: I'm happiest when I'm on stage

Entrepreneur: I want make my ideas a reality

Reporter: I love investigating and collecting stories

What Did We Miss?

If we left something out, jot it down!

Spotlight

Meet Sesame Workshop's Louis Henry Mitchell: The Artist Behind Your Favorite Furry Friends

By Alana Blumenstein

Even if you haven't met Louis Henry Mitchell, you've seen his work. His artistic creations live on in the form of characters on the iconic television show, Sesame Street. As Creative Director of Character Design at Sesame Workshop, the nonprofit behind Sesame Street, Louis has personally designed beloved faces like Kami, Wesley, Ji-Young, and Julia — the first Sesame Street Muppet with autism. His lifelong passion was born at the young age of six, when Jim Henson appeared on The Ed Sullivan Show.

"Sesame Street wasn't around yet, but Jim Henson's Muppets were," Mitchell recalls. "I just couldn't get enough of it."

It was a special televised program that opened Mitchell's eyes to the world of puppetry. Rather than simply perform, Jim Henson presented backstage secrets of the Muppets. It was standard for Henson to shake Sullivan's hand after each segment — but this time was different.

"He came out and still had Kermit on his arm, and I said, 'You mean a man was doing that?'"

"I didn't even get the whole thing out of my mouth before he said, 'Louis, you're aiming way too high. You're never gonna get a job like that,'" Mitchell recalls, adding that he was advised to aim lower to avoid disappointment.

"I was six years old," Mitchell says, adding that he never considered how Muppets became animated. "But when I saw that, it changed my life. Something snapped, that never snapped back. And that was the beginning of my career."

"I was nineteen and it broke my heart because, I thought: he's a teacher, he should know, right?"

So, fueled by his strong connection to Jim Henson and his creations, young Mitchell got to work. He made puppets out of Nerf Balls — and his sister's stolen socks. "They were so beautiful and colorful! It wasn't my fault," he jokes. "They were perfect for puppets."

He did everything he could to turn in his dream into reality, and his mother, Justa, saw that. "God bless my mother, she was always the hero of my life," Mitchell tributes, adding that she provided unconditional support.

In college, Mitchell decided it was time to take real steps toward his Sesame Street goals. With big dreams and an open heart, he gathered his portfolio materials and went to his favorite art professor for feedback.

Discouraged by his mentor, Mitchell went home with his shoulders hunched and his dreams crushed. He was ready to give up. But his mother wouldn't allow that. **"She said, 'What's wrong with you?'" Mitchell says. "So, I told her everything."**

And he did. He told her about the man on TV and the puppets he loved so much. He told her about his dreams of pursuing a career at his company. He told her how his professor had pronounced he had no chance. **"So, I might as well forget it," he remembers saying.**

"But my mom says: 'Tell me this. Does that teacher work for Sesame Street?' I said, 'No.' She says, 'So why are you listening to him?'"

Mitchell realized his mother was right. He put together a portfolio and brought it to the Jim Henson Company. That's where he met production receptionist Jennifer Lupinacci, who oversaw his application process and encouraged him to keep trying. But after eight months, Mitchell thought maybe his teacher was right.

"I promised myself: 'I'm going to drop off this portfolio one last time. If I don't get some kind of actual work, that means the teacher was right. And I might as well give it up.'"

When Mitchell dropped off his final portfolio, he was teary-eyed. But he knew it was time. He had to be realistic — even if that meant saying goodbye.

He arrived home later that day with a heavy heart. Absentmindedly, he checked his cassette answering machine tape when he noticed something new. A voicemail message from Sesame executive, Jim Mahon.

"He said, 'Louis, I heard that your portfolio was going around. It finally landed on my desk. And I really love what I see,'" Mitchell recalls his first job offer. **"I wore it out, listening over and over," Mitchell says.** It felt too good to be true.

133

At the meeting, Mitchell's portfolio was heavily complimented, and he was even equipped with guidelines to improve his future work. There was much learning to be done, but Mitchell had done it: he had earned his very first job at Sesame Street. And it was only the beginning of what has become a successful career.

Years later, Mitchell's dream job still feels unreal. "It never feels like work," he praises.

> "When your dream comes true, a dream of that magnitude, it's like, 'Wow, did I really get here?'"

As Creative Director of Character Design, there's no standard day at Sesame Workshop. Mitchell's work includes everything from designing new Sesame Street Muppets to drawing existing characters to directing photoshoots to attending company meetings to reviewing work by other artists and provides direction and guidance when needed. Some years, Mitchell even designs balloons and floats for the Macy's Thanksgiving Day Parade.

> "I'm immersed in my creativity," Mitchell says. "Whatever comes my way, I'm pretty much ready for. Even if I'm not ready, my heart's ready because I want to learn and bring it to whatever height I can."

One way Mitchell raises the height is by creating characters, like Julia, the first Sesame Street Muppet with autism. His inspiration began by coincidence at a school in Staten Island, where Mitchell volunteered with the kids on the spectrum, in and out of school. He dedicated most of his personal days on field trips, and even met some of their families on home visits. "I learned so much from that work," Mitchell says. "I got to see everything."

There was one participant he connected with most. **"This little girl just stole my heart,"** Mitchell recalls. "She was nonverbal, but she liked to put puzzles together. And sometimes she would have trouble, so, I would hold the next piece for her."

But the young girl did not know Mitchell was trying to help her. To her, it looked like he too, was having trouble.

So, Mitchell says, she took his hand, and they placed the pieces down together.

Eventually, Mitchell's personal days ran low, and his time with the program came to an end. On his last day, he prepared to say goodbye to the kids he had come to love. He stood by the door and watched them all dash out to head home — when one familiar face rushed by.

"She came out and passed me. And she stopped," Mitchell says. *"She looked around, she came back, and she took my hand, because I think she thought I was lost."*

It was a small gesture — but so incredibly large in Mitchell's heart. He knew then that he had made an impact that mattered. His connection with these kids would never be forgotten.

"When I was gifted the opportunity to design Julia, Sesame Workshop had been working on the initiative for many, many years," Mitchell explains, adding that they strived to truly understand a subject before creating initiatives around it. "They didn't know that I was volunteering at the school. It was like this beautiful serendipity that all came together perfectly."

Mitchell knows that one character cannot represent everyone. But alongside Dr. Jeanette Betancourt, who led the Autism initiative at Sesame Workshop, Mitchell hoped to showcase Julia's differences in a positive light.

"When you design a character, it's not so much what they look like, it's who they are," Mitchell says, explaining that the story-building comes long before sketching. *"So, I gave her a diamond shaped nose and that means she's a diamond in the rough."*

Julia's nose isn't her only unique feature. She has bright orange hair of human texture, to that would help her look more like a real little girl and instantly relatable. Her eyes are angled, slightly more than usual, because she sees the world differently than the Sesame Street Muppets before her. Most importantly to Mitchell, Julia never addresses the camera.

"She was never going to look into the camera and say, 'Hi, Welcome to Sesame Street,'" Mitchell says. "She was either going to be drawing or playing with her bunny, Fluffster, or doing something else, not engaging directly with the audience."

Julia's first appearance was a hit. "Everybody embraced her," Mitchell recalls. The episode closed with a song: *'We all have our own special things that make us who we are ...we may all be different but that's something that's worth praising.'*

When we embrace the things that make us different, we become the best versions of ourselves. But that takes confidence — something that takes time to build.

"I wasn't always confident," Mitchell admits, thinking back to his childhood as a shy kid. *"It's not a light switch. Practice what you love, keep trying, and don't be hard on yourself. The confidence is a byproduct of that commitment."*

Mitchell's suggestion? Be more like Grover. "Grover represents someone who, no matter how many mistakes he makes, has never doubted himself," Mitchell explains. "He just keeps going. He'll make another mistake, and another mistake, and another mistake. He only makes mistakes. That's all he does! But he's never doubted himself. And that's a good thing."

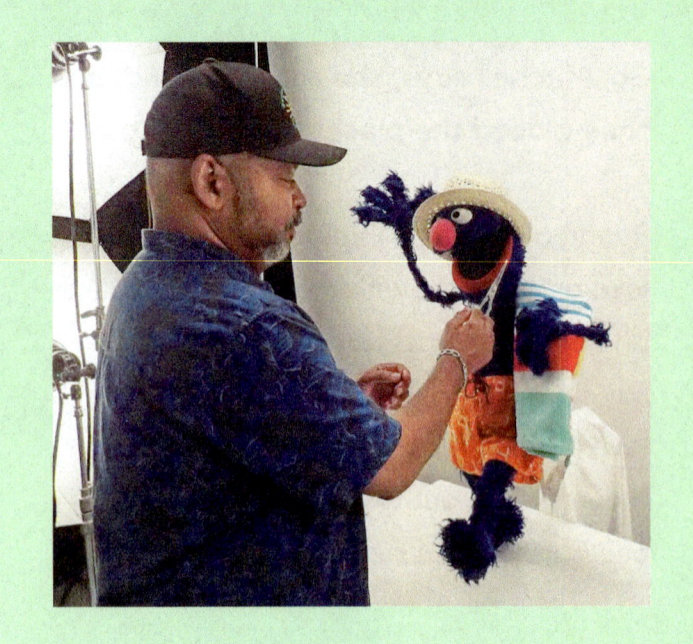

Much like our furry-friend Grover, Mitchell says we are all a work-in-progress. "For our entire lives, we never land. We always keep going," Mitchell says. "That means we can always learn something new; we can always keep growing."

Forget flaws, says Mitchell. Think of them as *assignments*. "That means now you're aware of the next thing you need to work on," he says, adding that the hard work will result in confidence. "I just wrapped myself around what I loved. And eventually it panned out."

Once upon a time, Mitchell was discouraged for having big dreams. Now, he is a cheerleader to those like him. "Not everybody wants to work for Sesame Street, but everybody has a dream," he says.

> "Look inside, follow your heart, and know that you don't decide what you're going to do in this life, you discover it."

Pay attention to the things that pique your interest, Mitchell advises. "Those are signals, those are signs, those are things that are giving you clues to who you are and what you're here for," he says.

There will always be doubters like Mitchell's past professor, but you get to choose the opinions that matter. "You have to be careful who you share your dreams with, because sometimes people don't understand," he warns.

> "Share your dreams with the people revealed to be in your corner; to be your tribe."

It can be disappointing when people don't believe in your ambitions. But Mitchell advises against holding grudges. "Those people show you what can happen to you when you don't embrace your life with that love," he says. "If I'm not mindful about how I walk my life, I can end up being like them."

No matter how far you feel from your inner child, Mitchell promises there's always a way to reconnect with the dreamer inside. It's all about love, says Mitchell. Loving yourself, loving others, loving the journey, and staying open to where it takes you.

Moments of doubt can feel overpowering, but they are just that: a moment. Hold on. Stay determined. Learn from Mitchell: those struggles will make sense in the end. **"I learned that they were not stumbling blocks: they were stepping-stones,"** he explains. **"I just had to look at it the right way. It's all about perception."**

There's a picture on Mitchell's desk of his greatest mentor. It is not Jim Henson, nor a Sesame Workshop executive, but a younger image of Mitchell himself. The six-year-old boy that fell in love with the Muppets; that dreamed of creating characters; that watched Jim Henson in awe on the Ed Sullivan Show.

> "I never want to forget who that six-year-old is," Mitchell says. "That's the real me."

That boy is why Mitchell is now living his dream. That boy is why Mitchell is fun and creative, and adventurous, and **kind.**

So, stay true to yourself, be kind to others, and when in doubt, take a note from Cookie Monster. "Cookie Monster is the greatest character on the face of the earth," Mitchell praises. "It's not the cookies. It's his personality. Everybody thinks the only thing he thinks about is eating cookies. But multiple times on the show, he's given away his last cookie."

In song, Cookie Monster explains the meaning of a friend: 'Maybe friend is someone you give up last cookie for,' Cookie sings. According to Mitchell, it's a quality that is not to be underestimated.

"You can love and be passionate about something, but still be sweet," Mitchell explains.

"You don't have to step over your friends or compete. And the thing about Cookie Monster is that he believes that if he gives someone one of his cookies, they're going to enjoy it as much as he does. But come on, is that loving or what?"

We could all stand to be a little bit more like our favorite monsters friends on Sesame Street; like Cookie Monster, who shares his greatest love with the world. Or Grover, who tries and tries and tries some more, unphased by mistakes, and unfamiliar with failure. Or even Julia, who embraces her differences like a true diamond in the rough.

Like Mitchell, don't let go of your childhood. Don't forget what fills your heart with joy. Your passions are not silly or stupid. They are courageous.

IT'S YOUR TURN!

Louis Henry Mitchell is known for designing Julia. Who will YOU create?

Your Turn!

Who is your character? Describe their personality. What makes them WHO they are?

A Day in the Life with American Girl's Executive Editor Jennifer Hirsch

Meet Jennifer Hirsch, Executive Editor at American Girl, as we discuss storytelling, creating beloved characters, and her typical day-in-the-life.

By Alana Blumenstein

1. Tell us a bit about yourself!

I have always loved children's books. Growing up in Berkeley, California, I read and reread my favorites: the original versions of Bambi, Black Beauty, The Black Stallion, The Lion, The Witch, and the Wardrobe, and so many others.

"I studied English literature in college, and my dream was always to write children's books for a living. (I also wanted to raise horses, but that didn't happen.)"

Now I live with my husband on an old farm outside Madison, Wisconsin. I have 3 kids, a dog, a cat, a horse, 12 chickens, and 16 huge goldfish that live in an old cattle trough.

2. How did you get started at American Girl? And why AG?

I started out as the company's copy editor in 1995. I read all the books, magazines, and catalogues, finding and fixing errors and inconsistencies.

"I caught a lot of mistakes, but once I didn't notice that our company phone number was wrong. A different company started getting our calls, wondering why so many people were calling to order dolls!"

Now I do developmental editing, which is helping authors develop their plots and characters and turn their ideas turn into a fun and satisfying story.

3. Your job is extremely creative. Growing up, was creativity a big part of your childhood?

Definitely! I started drawing as soon as I could hold a pencil, and once I learned how to read, I began to write and *illustrate* stories for fun. (Most of them were about horses.)

In high school, I wrote poetry and learned clay *sculpting* and how to make stained glass windows. I also played piano and guitar.

4. Today, as Executive Editor for American Girl, what's a day in the life for you?

A typical day usually includes a few meetings with other editors to talk about problems we're seeing in stories and how to fix them.

For example, perhaps a scene is boring, or a plot-line just isn't believable. I'll help the author figure out why, and how to fix the story to make it fun, interesting, and *plausible*. I might call or email the author to discuss the latest draft and offer suggestions for improving it.

I meet with the designers who create the dolls and toys that go with our books, and with our historian, who makes sure that everything is *accurate*.

"It's part of my job to make sure that our characters and their stories and worlds are presented accurately and consistently, whether it's a book, a movie, a video game, or a doll-stop-motion movie for YouTube."

I also meet with art directors to review illustrations for the books. If there are videos or games to go with the stories, I'll review those as they are being created.

5. You also develop products, like entertainment and education materials. What is that process like from idea to reality?

For entertainment such as movies and musicals, we work with outside partners who produce the entertainment. The partners find the scriptwriters and actors, and my job is to review the scripts, help choose the actors, and make sure the end product feels true to the original character.

Some aspects of the story might need to change to fit a different format, but the character's overall personality, situation, and themes must stay the same.

For example, Samantha must always be an orphan, and Julie must always stand up for equal rights for girls.

We look at what kids are learning in school in second, third, and fourth grade, and we focus on aspects of the story that tie into the curriculum—such as challenging vocabulary words or historical themes.

6. How do you come up with and pitch your ideas to the AG team? How do you find inspiration for each story?

Each year AG surveys girls and moms to find out what their interests, activities, and concerns are, and their answers help us decide what kinds of stories and characters to create.

For example, we learned that the 1980s are trendy because it's the era many parents grew up in, so we created Courtney, our 1980s girl.

We learned that girls love cheerleading and want to know what it's like to live with a disability, so our 2020 Girl of the Year, Joss, takes up competitive cheer and wears a hearing aid because she is partially deaf.

Courtesy of American Girl. PAC-MAN™ &©BANDAI NAMCO Entertainment Inc.

Our authors and editors often draw on personal experience. For example, the character Julie is growing up in San Francisco in the 1970s, which is very near where I grew up and the same decade that both the author, Megan McDonald, and I grew up in. So many of Julie's experiences were **inspired** by things that happened to Megan or me. And some of Rebecca's experiences also happened to her author, Jacqueline Greene—such as having to make Christmas decorations in fourth grade, even though she was Jewish!

7. What makes a good story? What are the must-have elements to make it work?

"It needs a good conflict—something for readers to care about so that they will root for the main character. Without that, stories are boring."

The conflict must be believable within the world of the story, and it must be something that really matters to the main character. And the main character must solve the **conflict** in a convincing way.

8. You like to talk to kids in your stories, rather than down to them. I so admire that about you. How do you ensure all of your stories have that kid-like quality?

It's essential to respect your audience. Kids are smarter than most adults realize, and much more honest than adults are.

"Children are also more in touch with their gut feelings—they know when something isn't right, even if they don't always say so out loud. If a writer is talking down to them, kids will know it."

I look for children's authors who write with intelligence and honesty, and who can "channel" a child's voice and viewpoint in a convincing way so that to the reader, it seems like the character having the experiences in the story is a real person.

Writers can only do that if they respect kids and understand—or remember—what it's like to see the world through a child's eyes.

9. What is your favorite part about working at American Girl?

My favorite part is the constant creativity. Whether it's creating new characters, new stories about old characters, or new types of content such as quizzes or musicals, or movies, I'm never bored and always challenged.

"The characters we create feel so real to me, I can hear their voices in my head. I know them so well that it's easy for me to tell an author or scriptwriter, "Julie would never say that!" or "Felicity wouldn't do that—but she might do this." I know my characters as well as I know my own kids!"

10. What has been the hardest thing about your job?

The hardest thing is getting good stories written FAST. We usually have only 3-6 months to write each book, so that it will be printed and ready to go when the doll is sold. That might sound like a lot of time, but it's not!

That's one reason the editors sometimes have to help the author finish a story or write the final draft—because the author needs to start writing the next book in the series!

11. What would you suggest to those looking to get started as an editor or creator for a company like American Girl?

To become an editor, you'll need a college degree in English, history, journalism, psychology, or a similar field that teaches you how to research, read deeply and write.

To become a writer, you should write often and try writing a lot of different things: stories, nonfiction, quizzes, and plays.

Then find publishers who publish that kind of writing and submit your work or apply for a job.

If you're rejected, don't give up! Most of us were rejected at first, but if you have talent and love what you're doing, keep trying. Any time you have the chance to write for a school paper, yearbook, or writing contest, do it.

"If you don't, then just write your own stories. You will get better and better the more you write. Also, think about why you love your favorite books and authors. Could you write like that? Try it!"

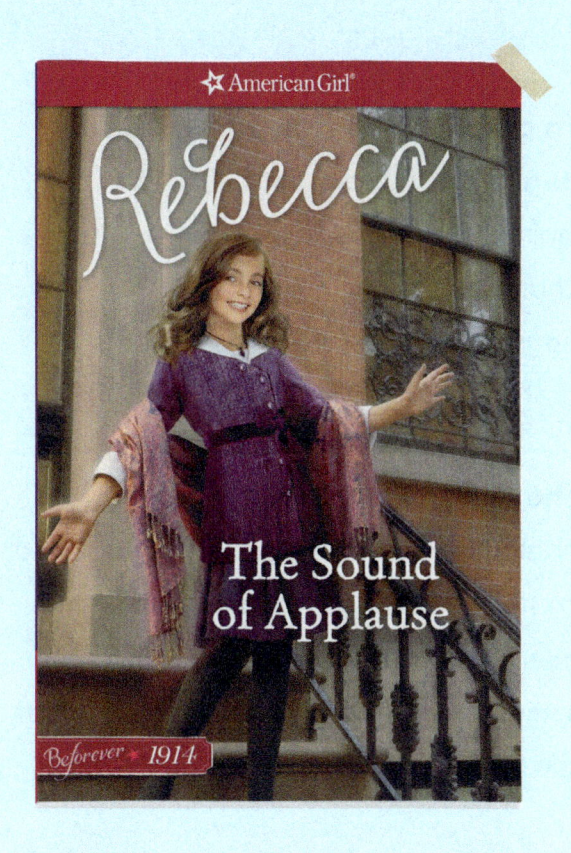

12. What advice would you give to your younger self?

Listen to other people's advice about your writing. Try doing it their way. Only then can you decide if it's good advice or not. But even if you decide their way isn't right for you, you'll still learn something that will help make you a better writer or editor.

13. For a child at home who is learning to write, what advice would you give them on storytelling? What are the steps to creating a good character or story arc?

To create a story arc, you need a beginning, middle, and end—and the main character, or **protagonist**, must change from beginning to end. The beginning is the setup, the way the protagonist starts out.

The middle is what happens to challenge the protagonist: a problem or conflict that the protagonist must overcome in order to achieve or gain something s/he wants. This is the bulk of the story.

The ending shows how the protagonist has changed because of these experiences.

For example: In A Christmas Carol, Scrooge starts out **greedy** and selfish at the beginning.

In the middle, he has experiences and visions that force him to reflect on his greed and selfishness and the people he has hurt, including himself—and he **vows** to change his ways. The final scene shows how Scrooge has changed to become **generous** and caring.

14. My siblings prefer to read comic books and/or listen to audiobooks.

What do you think is the importance of encouraging a love of reading — of all kinds?

Reading and listening to stories takes you to other places—real and imaginary, in the past, present, and future.

"It takes you into the mind of another person, or even an animal! In short, reading and listening to stories exercise the imagination. For this reason, I believe that it's the best way to understand our larger world—everything that's out there beyond the world of our own personal experience."

15. What advice would you give a struggling reader?

Try another type of book, such as a picture book or a comic book. There are some wonderful graphic novels and heavily illustrated novels like Captain Underpants that can make the transition to independent reading easier.

"My brother hated reading until he found the Peanuts comic books about Charlie Brown and Snoopy. These are legitimate children's literature—don't let anyone tell you they're not!"

Ingredients For A Story

1. The Story Arc

Every story needs a plot! Does your story have a...

- [ ] Beginning
- [ ] Middle
- [ ] End

2. Conflict

Why do we root for the protagonist?

3. Emotion

Your story should be written with honesty and feeling. The characters should feel REAL to you.

Tip: Write, write, write, and write some more! You'll get better with every word :)

Watch this video for even more story tips!

SCAN ME

Your Turn!

My Story Recipe

Genre:

What kind of story is it?
(Ex: fantasy, romance, action, etc.)

Title:

Every story needs one!

The Big Idea:

What is my main focus? What message am I trying to get across?

Emotions:

What feelings will inspire my writing?
Ex: happiness, sadness, frustration, etc.)

IT'S YOUR TURN!

All stories have an arc - a beginning, a middle, and an end. Using your character, plan your story's plot.

BEGINNING: How does the protagonist start out?

MIDDLE: What conflict does the protagonist face?

END: How is the story resolved?

Are You a Kit or a Ruthie?

We'll reveal which best friend you are!

I am...
- A) Curious, clever, & practical
- B) Romantic, cheerful, & kind

I love to wear...
- A) Nothing too flouncy...
- B) Ruffles, ruffles, ruffles!

Pick a story to read.
- A) The Adventures of Robinhood
- B) Grimm's Fairy Tales

Pick a hobby.
- A) Baseball and/or writing
- B) Dancing and/or horseback riding

My biggest flaw is...
- A) I'm too proud to accept help
- B) My head gets stuck in the clouds...

My hero is...
- A) A famous historical figure
- B) A famous actress

People praise me for...
- A) My can-do attitude & creative solutions
- B) Being a positive & loyal friend

If you have mostly...

A) You're Kit!

Like Kit, you don't beat around the bush. You are direct, practical and determined. Your curiosity makes you are an excellent problem solver, and an even better reporter. Just remember to keep that can-do attitude, and that asking for help makes you strong.

P.S. Not all reporters write articles. You can investigate every day by asking questions, active listening, and writing down your thoughts in a trusted journal.

B) You're Ruthie!

Like Ruthie, you are a dreamer. You love using your imagination, telling stories, and finding the light in any situation. You are a great listener and can make anyone smile, which makes you the best friend ever. Just remember: you make a difference every day just by being you.

P.S. Every fairy tale was new, once upon a time. Next time you're in dreamland, try writing your own! Imagine a faraway land... where would you begin?

Bruce Lanoil Plays Pretend for a Living

Growing up, Bruce Lanoil's imagination took him on countless adventures. Now, the Muppeteer is using that same creativity to light a spark in children around the world.

By Alana Blumenstein

Growing up, Bruce Lanoil's imagination took him on countless **adventures**. Now, the Muppeteer is using that same creativity to light a spark in children around the world. Lanoil's performances have helped bring to life **beloved** characters from The Muppets, The Wubbulous World of Dr. Seuss, Dr. Dolittle, Dinosaurs, Where the Wild Things Are, and Jack Frost, among others. In childhood, Lanoil struggled to fit in. Yet his greatest strength was believing in himself.

"I knew what was going on inside of me," he says. "All of these things that I saw as a kid, unbelievably, I **manifested** in my life."

Long before his days as a Muppeteer, Lanoil had a special talent. He could turn anything — from the sugary cereals at breakfast to the cartoons they watched at night — into a moment to remember. Born by the countryside of New Jersey, Lanoil's humor came in handy — especially in the company of his parents.

"Families can get tense and my family... they all grew up in one-bedroom apartments in Brooklyn," Lanoil shares. "All my dad's parents **emigrated**, and so they were trying to fit in. Everybody was just trying to be who they weren't."

Whether he was narrowly avoiding trouble or simply sharing happiness; both afforded the same result. By the time Lanoil was finished, it hardly mattered what had been said or done: his parents were on the floor with laughter.

"I found everybody's sense of **humor**. I listened, and I saw what was missing," he explains, detailing how comedy could cure his family's anger and frustration.

Lanoil in The Wubbulous World of Dr. Seuss.

"I **defused** a lot of situations, by seeing where I could **inject** something lighter for everybody. And I built on that."

Though Lanoil had conquered life at home, the outside world was a different story. Wherever he went, he never quite felt like he fit in. "We were a Jewish family, and we were one of only a couple," he says. "Then I grew up very heavy, and there was just labeling very quickly."

Kids made first-glance **impressions**, says Lanoil, leading his choice of friends to be limited, and his self-esteem to suffer. But the friends he made, he **cherished** for life.

Lanoil with actor John Cleese and Daffy Duck.

"I had a best friend named Greg Metcalf, and I was fat, and he was skinny," he laughs. "I don't even know why he was my friend, because my self-esteem was just not there."

With his friends, his imagination truly began to thrive. "We had an imaginative friendship where we pretended everything," he shares, recalling how his love of Star Trek led to a particularly special birthday. Eight-year-old Lanoil was so inspired that he re-created the show with his own group of classmates. The night was magical 'til the end, as each friend 'beamed down' until all that remained were him and Greg.

"But it was that kind of stuff, where we would just build worlds and make forts in the snow," Lanoil reminisces. "That's where I lived. And that's where I was alive was in these pretend worlds with my closest friends."

As he grew older, his love for pretend led him to pursue acting. Yet time after time, his auditions were met with rejection. Lanoil **contemplated** quitting, but he couldn't bear to leave his childhood passions behind. He found his answer in puppetry.

"When I was in puppets, I was totally free with my sense of humor to do anything I wanted to do. I wasn't **confined** by what you saw, because I could do anything with my hand," he explains.

"So, all of that studying that I did as a kid really paid off as a young adult and into my professional career."

The work was meaningful in more ways than one, as Lanoil was embraced alongside the original cast and crew of The Muppets.

Lanoil (second from left) piloting a four-person puppet.

With it came a lot of work and he rehearsed as much as he could, learning useful skills like improvisation and strengthening his hand-eye coordination. But rather unexpectedly, Lanoil found his heroes had somehow become his friends.

"There's nothing like it, to be a part of something bigger than yourself. Then you understand why we're all here on the earth and how we are interconnected," he says. "There's no black and white, there's all these colors of gray. And we all live in them, no matter who we are. That's what The Muppets were in that moment. Everybody in the audience was united."

When he filmed Dinosaurs, a Henson company production that used ground-breaking animatronic puppets, it was shortly after Jim Henson had passed. The cast felt entirely lost without him.

The movie was beautiful, says Lenoil, and Brian Henson invited him to return for another project. For the first time, Frank Oz, Jerry Nelson, Richard Hunt, Dave Goelz, would play their beloved characters without the man that started it all.

When Lenoil entered the room, the group seemed utterly despondent. Then something magical happened. "They started going through the script, and then they started joking around, and then they just started playing, and then they started remembering, and then they started laughing ... and the script got funnier and funnier, and the room just lifted up," he recalls.

"And I saw who they were, and what Jim was all about, and this ensemble, who are just grown men playing their hearts out in honor and being true to who they were."

The moment, which Lenoil calls mind-blowing, ignited a feeling of pride unlike any other. "That was my entry point to say, these are, why the Muppets are who they are, why they are so beloved, and why they will always go on because of the people who take the torch and run up the hill," he says. "And just want to show the world that we belong, we are together, we are different. And yet we are a family."

IT'S YOUR TURN!

All characters have a unique look. What does your character LOOK like?

Your Turn!

MAKE MINI MONSTER PUPPETS!

Watch our tutorial!

SCAN ME

MATERIALS
- 4x6 Index Card
- Pipe Cleaner
- Googly Eyes
- Feathers
- Pom Poms
- Crayons/Markers

Learning through Play with the LEGO Foundation's Bo Stjerne Thomsen

From Denmark to Mexico to the United States to Austria, Bo Stjerne Thomsen has created playful experiences all around the globe.

By Alana Blumenstein

Bo Stjerne Thomsen, Vice President of Learning through Play at the LEGO Foundation, can create a playful experience from just about anything. Growing up in a small farm in Denmark, Thomsen relied on nature for entertainment.

"One of the main things my parents did in childhood was provide access to stimulation in the environment around me," he says, adding he was taught early on to explore independently.

Though they did not have a lot of resources, Thomsen had the opportunity to engage with books, music, outdoor sports, and farm animals.

The freedom to wander (and wonder) allowed him infinite opportunities to use his imagination — something he still appreciates in his daily life today.

From Denmark to Mexico to the United States to Austria, Thomsen has traveled the world. After receiving a master's degree in design, architecture and engineering, and a PhD on performative learning environments, he started his career at the MIT Media Lab, before moving onto the LEGO Learning Institute. "I was really inspired by that work with research and understanding human psychology and education and technology," he notes, emphasizing how adding play to education can make a difference.

"There's so much need for play, particularly right now."

Today, he serves Vice President of Learning through Play at the LEGO Foundation. **"I collect all the fantastic evidence we have on how children learn through playful experiences,"** he explains.

"I help inform our decisions around what kind of activities to do, but also the products and experiences to help inform with our research."

As an educator across the globe, Thomsen teaches how to enhance play in our daily lives. **Part of that magic happens in LEGO's very own LEGO Idea Studio, the creative workspace behind several of their key experiences and inventions.**

"With the LEGO bricks, we can build anything we can possibly imagine as if they were glued and yet they can easily be taken apart of reconfigured into a new idea," the description reads.

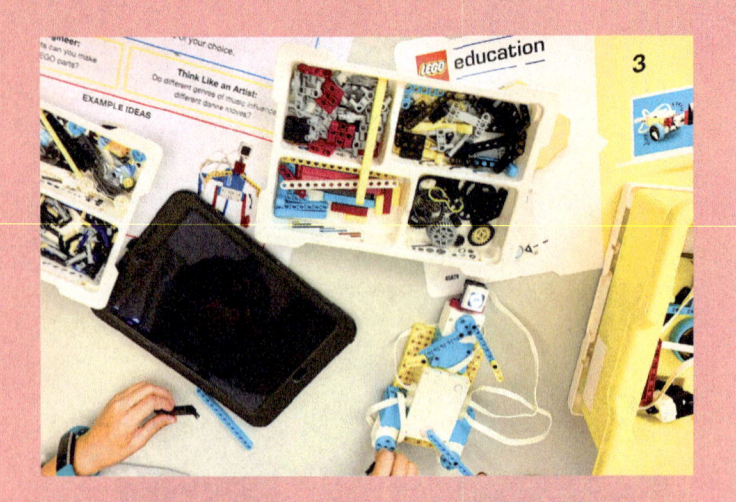

"When we do this, we are not only creating, but also evaluating, reflecting, and recreating to achieve new possibilities. We learn through play in a self-motivated and fun way."

Thomsen has experienced the Idea Studio's community building firsthand. **"The best way to encourage hands-on learning is to do it ourselves,"** he says of the studio's purpose, adding that in addition to product testing, the studio hosts guest demonstrations. **"The idea is to inspire people to all the different ways you can create toys and learning materials."**

If there's anything Thomsen's learned, it's that the world of play contains endless possibilities, and there's an infinite number of ways to express your ideas.

LEGO creations are built just to be built again — a process Thomsen practices on repeat. "The most important lesson, I think, is that learning as playing is a process of testing and trying out things, particularly things you really enjoy doing," he says of the hands-on process. **"It's really about your passions and your interests, and then expressing ideas that are meaningful to you."**

Thomsen's aware of the stigma behind play. But he would argue that learning through play engages the mind more than a typical school day.

"You are so deeply engaged when you're playing; when you have things in your hands," he explains.

"I think sometimes we think about play as something that's very frivolous, but it's so inherently serious, because you actually develop confidence, problem solve, and you're able to come up with lots of different ideas."

There's lots of different ways for parents and kids to use LEGOs, from instructed sets to open-ended free play. Each have their own benefits. "Some children really appreciate having a box, knowing what to do, starting from one point and building a model," he says. "Other children would really like to have it open ended. I think the starting point is to be open-minded and to start with something specific and structured but try to create a little uncertainty around it."

Thomsen insists there's no one path to becoming a designer at LEGO — or to succeeding in life. "What's interesting is they don't come with any specific degree as a background," he says of the team of almost 300 designers. "You can come as a craftsman, or you can come as an engineer, or as a designer, or as an artist. I think the most important thing is if you have been doing projects that you're passionate about." This could include anything from designing home furniture to filming stop motion videos to testing out potential new products.

That passion and curiosity is the key behind LEGO's success — and is what makes Thomsen's work so special.

"What I find most interesting about the work is really to see what children do when engaged in playful experiences," he says. "Developing the LEGO products is really, really motivating, because we are truly able to make a difference."

For any skeptics out there, Thomsen emphasizes the benefits of a playful approach to learning. "You get more creative and collaborative at the same time," he says of interactive, experiential learning.

"I think it's very important to keep that optimism. Play is your opportunity to create your own life, undefined by who other people think you are."

Your Turn!

IT'S YOUR TURN!

Now it's time to build the world. What does the SETTING look like? Where is the story located?

Books are a uniquely portable MAGIC.

Steven King

For Connie Guglielmo, Editor-in-Chief of CNET, Every Day is an Adventure

As a young reader in Brooklyn, Connie Guglielmo never imagined her path would lead to tech. Today, the self-proclaimed adventurer is the Editor-in-Chief of CNET.

By Alana Blumenstein

For Connie Guglielmo, Editor-in-Chief of CNET, every day is an adventure. The veteran tech journalist, who now serves at the world's leader in tech product reviews, news, and how-tos, sees everything, good and bad, as an opportunity to learn something new.

"If you're learning something, and you're not hurting people in the process, that's an adventure," she says.

"I wish that when I was a kid, people had reminded me of that."

As a child, Guglielmo's search for adventure led her to storytelling. In her childhood home in Brooklyn, she was often found hidden in closets, with her nose deep in a book. **"I used to hide in closets, with my flashlight, reading,"** she recalls, detailing how stories changed her worldview with new ideas and perspectives.

> "I'm not an expert in everything, but I have the confidence that I can learn anything if I put my mind to it. Maybe not become an engineer or chemist overnight, but ... I don't fear it's beyond my can."

Guglielmo interviewing actor Edward Norton.

When it was time for college, Guglielmo set her eyes on being a reporter. The field was unheard of in her household. Shaking her head, Guglielmo remembers her mother's shock at the news.

"She was like, 'Why would you want to be a paparazzi?' I'm like, 'No, it's not a paparazzi. It's different than that.' That just wasn't in their dynamic," she explains. Yet she was determined. Just as reading allowed her to escape to new worlds, storytelling allowed her to create her own.

Whatever she read or wrote, she couldn't help but notice the struggles of her mother, who had immigrated from Italy. Her father, who had Brooklyn roots, had met her mother while traveling in Europe. Guglielmo describes how her mother was unfairly dismissed by others. "She had a heavy accent, and people treated her badly," she says. "Even in a place like New York, where there are many different people and accents."

Still, Guglielmo carries that with her, naming it as her motivation for being a journalist. "I don't like seeing people lose," she says. Yet she never would have imagined her path would lead to tech.

"If you told me when I was in college, I would become a technology journalist, I would have laughed at you," she admits. "I'm not mechanically inclined."

Guglielmo, who attended UCLA undergrad, was not introduced to technology until college while working in the school newsroom. "There wasn't this thing called 'tech,'" she says, adding that students primarily used pen and paper to write stories before transferring to typewriters and, later, devices like the IBM Electric.

CNET crowd shot following Guglielmo's interview with John Travolta (center).

> "After that, I happened to be just at the right place at the right time as these technologies were introduced to the world," she says.

After graduation, Guglielmo got her first job working PR at Ashton Tate, a company known for creating one of the world's first online databases. She received her Master's in Communication at Stanford University, where her interest in tech continued to expand.

In a field of few women, she began writing about the internet and the 'World Wide Web,' and penned early stories about up-and-coming companies like Amazon and eBay.

"All of that was new," Guglielmo says. "With tech, there was a small world that started in Silicon Valley, and then it has expanded to everything that you use today."

But her upward climb soon came to a halt. "After 9/11, the media industry in the country kind of collapsed," she remembers. She explains that many publications shut down, leaving writers like her unemployed. So, along with seven other journalists, she created her own: AGoodPeople.com.

With no funding, they co-edited each other's columns and learned how to build a website from scratch.

"It was good for us to all have this group camaraderie," Guglielmo reflects. "As the group was around the country, and technology allowed us to share and write stories together, we got media attention."

The attention was enough to land many of them jobs, and Guglielmo went off to become a financial reporter at Bloomberg. "What it showed me was that if you can be creative and inventive, you can get through anything," she says of the time.

"I'm friends with those people, many of them to this day, because when you're going through a difficult time you remember the people who helped you. Networking is important in any industry in the world. But having friends that can share experiences with you can get you through any period."

With a liberal arts background, Guglielmo's entire career is built off a dedication to learn. Her unfamiliarity with tech products not only taught her to be curious, but to write articles that anyone could understand.

> "Read a lot. Don't be afraid to ask questions. Don't be afraid to know what you don't know," Guglielmo advises.

> "If someone explains it to you, and you still don't understand, do you know what the bravest question is? 'I still don't understand, can you explain it again.'"

In a field underrepresented by women, Guglielmo's ability to look at technology from an outside perspective has pushed her to succeed where others haven't. "We have proven at CNET, there's a way to do that. We are profitable newsroom, and I have expanded my staff over the past six years, which a lot of news organizations can't say that they've done," she says, crediting her diverse team. "But it goes back to being creative and thinking about it in the long term, not just the short term."

For Connie Guglielmo, every day is an adventure: because she makes an active choice to make it so. **"Doing and learning just makes you a more interesting and compelling person,"** says Guglielmo, whose mantra is to **learn something new every year.**

Whether she is practicing the piano or weaving a pin loom, that mindset has pushed her to grow in her career and in life.

> It's good to be a well-rounded person," she says. "Otherwise, time just passes. What's the fun in that?"

Your Turn!

IT'S YOUR TURN!

Connie taught us that learning is an adventure. Given the topic of your story, what must you research?

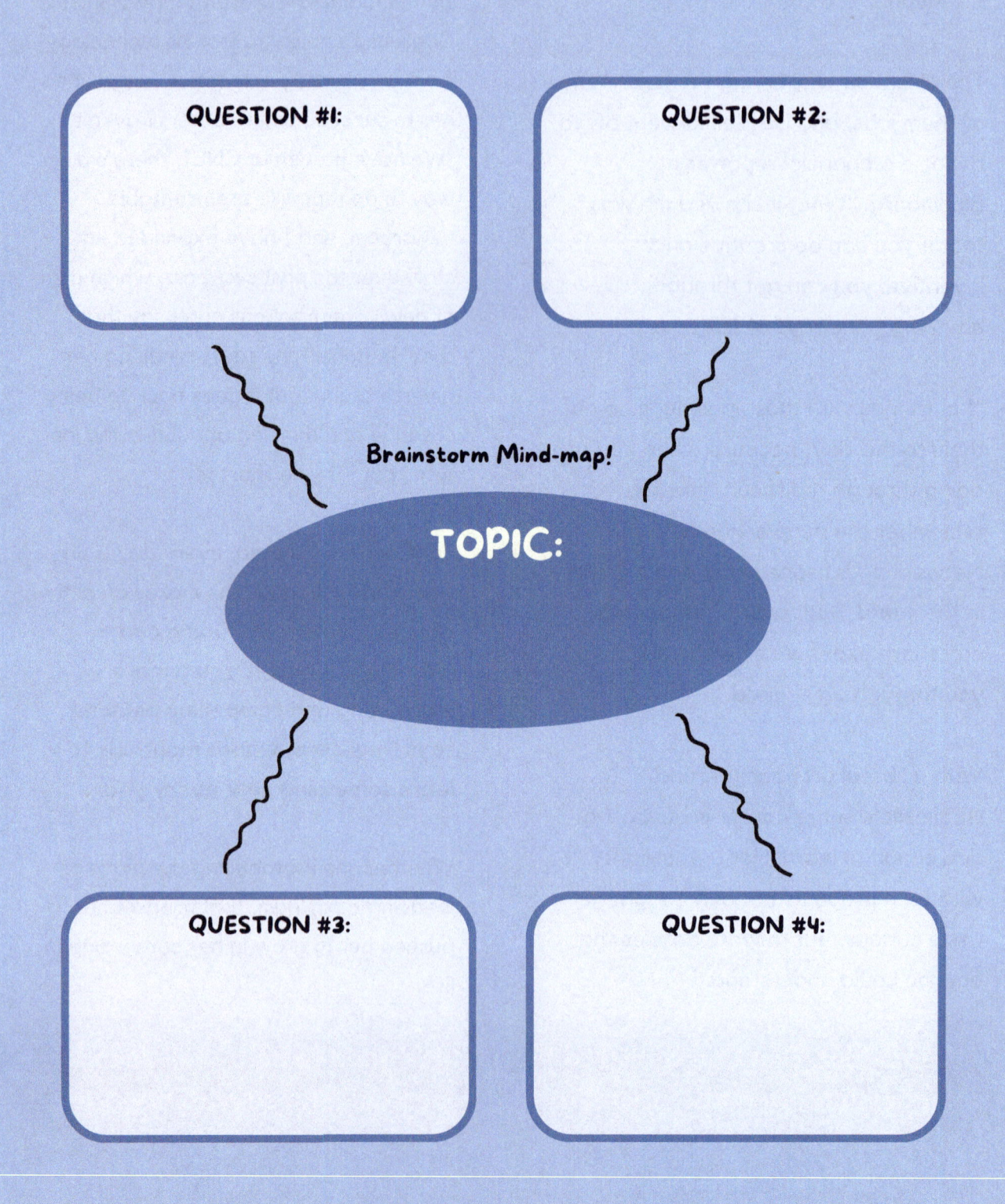

QUESTION #1:

QUESTION #2:

Brainstorm Mind-map!

TOPIC:

QUESTION #3:

QUESTION #4:

The Five W's

Five questions to help you focus your research. We'll use Connie as example!

WHO is your character?

Connie Guglielmo, Editor-in-Chief of CNET. She is a tech journalist, serving at the world's leader in tech product reviews, news, and how-tos.

WHAT is your story?

How Connie evolved from a young reader in Brooklyn to becoming the veteran tech leader she is today.

WHERE is the setting?

At CNET, and worldwide, as Connie travels the world telling stories.

WHY is this happening?

Connie uses her voice to make a difference - inspired by her mother's struggles as an immigrant. She sees everything, good and bad, as an opportunity to learn something new and is unafraid to ask questions.

WHEN does your story take place?

From her childhood, until NOW!

My Sources

Introducing the KidsRead2Kids 'FACT' Method:

F: Factual

Is the information supported by evidence? Does the article cite sources? Does the information match other research?

TIP: Gather at least four sources to ensure your information is accurate. Check the domain name. Aim for .edu or .gov.

A: Angle

Is the writer sharing an opinion or personal bias? Is this an ad or a researched article?

TIP: Trust your gut. If it looks off, move on. There are lots of sources out there. You don't need to settle.

C: Current

Is the information current? When was the article written or last updated?

TIP: Look for articles written or updated in the last 5-10 years.

T: Trustworthy

Who are the author and publisher? Do they have professional experience in the field?

TIP: Credentials are qualifications of the author. For example, their past education and work history.

NOW YOU'RE READY!

Pretend you are interviewing your main character. What must you learn? Write your questions and answers below.

Dr. Amanda Gummer Credits Play for Her Success

Dr. Amanda Gummer, founder of Good Play Guide, is the go-to expert on child development, toys and play. But the secret to her success may surprise you.

By Alana Blumenstein

Growing up in a playful household, Dr. Amanda Gummer, founder of Dr. Gummer's Good Play Guide, never felt pressured to be perfect. Her family viewed learning for what it was: an opportunity for growth — and fun.

"I was very lucky to have a very playful childhood," Dr. Gummer shares. "My dad used to sell toys and my mom made everything into a game."

Today, she is widely known as the go-to expert on child development, toys, and play. When it comes to education, she hopes parents and children will foster the same joyous experience.

"I love watching kids play," Dr. Gummer says. "I like the fact that it's not stigmatized. Kids do it at their own pace in their own way."

Though she's been researching and working with families for nearly 20 years, she adds that play still excites her. **"I never cease to be amazed with how imaginative kids can be."**

With a PhD in psychology from The University of Sheffield, she has founded three organizations, including Good Toy Guide Ltd and FUNdamentals. In September 2014, she combined the two into Fundamentally Children, now known as Dr. Gummer's Good Play Guide.

Today they are the UK's leading source of expert, independent advice on child development and play. She is also the author of Play: Fun ways to help your children develop in the first five years, published in May 2015.

But Dr. Gummer wasn't always a child development expert. Originally, her studies focused on neuropsychology and how the brain works. After receiving her PhD in 2000, Dr. Gummer spent time working for a charity for vulnerable families and later, lived in Hong Kong. There, she worked for an educational organization that followed a learning through play approach.

Those few years passed quickly, and before she knew it, she had two daughters. In that moment, her fascination with child development was born. "I realized that I was just fascinated," Dr. Gummer says.

"On paper, I should have found parenting really easy," she notes, regarding her expansive experience. "And for a number of reasons I didn't. And that really piqued my interest because I was like, Well, you know, why am I not finding it easy? What are they doing? Why are they doing it?"

So, Dr. Gummer returned to her books and got up to date with her research. With her two young kids, she moved back to the UK.

"I was wondering what I was going to do with my life," Dr. Gummer shares. She says she turned to her father, John Nicholas, for inspiration. Nicholas worked in the toy industry as a sales agent. His company had a product that was succeeding in Japan and they wondered about the UK. They planned to test a focus group, and Nicholas turned to his daughter for help.

Looking back, Dr. Gummer credits that experience for her career now. "I did that just as almost a favor, and really enjoyed it and found it really interesting," she says.

Though Dr. Gummer is active in the Toy industry, she emphasizes that her primary passion lies with more than toys. "I think good toys are important," she clarifies. **"But it's the playfulness that they bring rather than the toys themselves."**

For Dr. Gummer, the best part of her job is demonstrating the power of play. She says she's happiest seeing that "penny dropping moment" when people discover that play is good.

"For me, I know that when that happens, that's going to change a child's life," she says. "That's the bit that makes my heart sing."

On a personal note, Dr. Gummer's biggest inspirations are close to home. "My inspirations definitely come from my family," she says. "My grandparents were always good for a game." Dr. Gummer hopes to keep play in her family for future generations — starting with her two daughters. "My kids, I just want to have a playful life and certainly a playful childhood."

Dr. Gummer's greatest strengths come from her biggest struggles.

In addition to making anything into a game, she says her real-life superpower came from overcoming her natural introversion and fear of public speaking. "People seem to like listening to some of the stuff I have to say now, and I've had to get over my natural introversion," she says.

At first, she found herself looking down towards the ground and struggling to speak. Though it was a difficult process, Dr. Gummer says it's worth it.

"I've done it because I really believe in what I'm saying," she says, adding that she grew empowered from the experience. "That is probably ... one of the things I'm proudest of because it definitely didn't come easy."

Dr. Gummer tells KidsRead2Kids she shares the same favorite novel: L.M. Montgomery's Anne of Green Gables. "I just think she's brilliant," she gushes. "It was all just lovely." She says her favorite reading spot is in her parent's holiday chalet by the sea.

"You just sit on the sofa and [there's] just nothing between you and ... the sea."

Currently, her reading list includes The Power by Naomi Alderman, Becoming by Michelle Obama, and I am Malala by Christina Lamb and Malala Yousafzai. In her free time, Dr. Gummer enjoys swimming and water sports, travel, gardening, and being with friends and family.

Dr. Gummer's mission is to make the world a more playful place. In the future, she hopes more parents and teachers will follow in her footsteps.

"I'm living proof that it's a good thing," she says. "If you've got two ways to do things, choose the fun way because, why wouldn't you?"

IT'S YOUR TURN!

Your Turn!

Dr. Gummer taught us that play IS learning. Using your character and plot outline, write and/or draw your story.

Use at least eight vocabulary words from our collection. (See page 213.)

I am not afraid of storms, for I am learning how to sail my ship.

Little Women

Louisa May Alcott

5 Questions with Cookie-Preneur Collette Divitto of Collettey's Cookies

1. Tell us about yourself!

Hi, I'm Collette, I was born in 1990, and the founder of Collettey's. I was born in Boston, and I went to college at Clemson University in South Carolina. I have loved baking since I was four years old.

2. What inspired you to turn your passion for baking into a career?

In high school, I was having a hard time. I had no friends and I got bullied a lot. I don't like to feel down on myself. So, my mom signed me up for baking classes, and I started baking every weekend. That's when I realized my love for baking was more than a hobby.

After college, I was excited about jobs. I went on 14 job interviews.

> I got rejected 14 times. No one would hire me because of my disability. I was told I wasn't the "right fit" for the company.

It's very sad, and that's why I left to start my own business in 2016.

3. What's it like running your own cookie company, where you aim to change the world — one cookie at a time?

I love having my own company and being my own boss. It makes me feel confident in myself and secure in my job. My cookie company has six flavors of our cookies that are all my own recipe. It's not always easy and we work pretty hard a lot.

But I love what I do so sometimes it doesn't feel like work. But other time we get so busy that we have no time for ourselves or our family or friends.

My favorite thing is creating jobs for people with disabilities and empowering them at work!

I also have a nonprofit where I teach people with disabilities how to succeed in life. My teaching is about how to become an entrepreneur, how to start your own business, and how to become independent and empowered.

4. What advice would you give to those like you?

Love what you do. Be willing to work hard. Also, what I would say is to not focus on your disabilities, but to focus on your abilities. Focus on what's best for yourself. Lastly, I love saying this: no matter who you are, you can make a big difference in the world.

5. Out of all of your amazing cookies, which is your favorite?

Cinnamon chocolate chip! Because it is my money maker and everyone loves them!

IT'S YOUR TURN!

Your Turn!

Collette showed us that our story is never over - even in the face of rejection. What lesson has your character taken away from this journey? How have they changed?

James Longman's Late Late Show Success Began with Stories

From listening to stories as a child to creating live skits on *The Late Late Show with James Corden*, Longman shares the secrets to Executive Producing the Emmy-winning show.

By Alana Blumenstein

James Longman, Co-Executive Producer of *The Late Late Show with James Corden*, doesn't often get asked about his childhood. Yet the 2-time Emmy winner credits it for his success today. On a Zoom call with KidsRead2Kids, he explains his love for diving into new worlds.

"My parents always read to me in bed … and it just seeped into me," he shares. "My job now is storytelling, and back then it was just reading stories."

Growing up in Chigwell, Essex, Longman's days were filled with lots and lots of books. "I was always nose in a book," he says, adding that the smell of books still excites him.

His favorites include British Classics like The Chronicles of Narnia by C.S. Lewis, The Magic Faraway Tree by Enid Blyton, and stories by Roald Dahl. Nothing excited Longman more than fictional, fantastical worlds that lived deep in adventure.

Longman behind-the-scenes on set.

"They're so rich in storytelling and characters," he explains, adding that it helps readers immerse themselves in the story. "You want to know where they go, which is so vital when you're reading it to be hooked in."

Longman's love of books encouraged him to write stories of his own. As a young student, Longman remembers how one teacher particularly helped him. "Our English teacher would act everything out and keep you involved and enamored with it all," he says. Though writers like Shakespeare can be difficult to follow, Longman's teacher brought their stories to life.

Longman's passion for stories led him to pursue movies, TV, and film. He began studying at Sunderland University, where he learned camera, audio, writing, and producing skills. When Longman was 21, he got his first job in television.

He's been hooked on the industry ever since. "Once I got my first job in TV, I realized that I liked being behind the camera," he says. "I liked producing things. I liked pulling everything together and creating that way."

Getting hired in the entertainment industry is a difficult feat, Longman admits. Yet, he persevered, by writing "loads and loads of letters" at a time before email. When one letter landed at MTV, five months later, he was offered an internship.

To survive in the business, Longman lists positivity, teamwork, and a good work ethic as essential qualities.

"Life is tough, and work can be tough," he says, emphasizing that it's important not to be an obstacle. "If you have a positive attitude, it can exude positivity in other people."

Longman and Tom Cruise on set.

Longman, James Corden and the cast of *Thor: Ragnarok*.

Today, as Co-Executive Producer for *The Late Late Show with James Corden*, Longman works as a professional problem solver. "If they've got a problem, they come to me," he says. "That allows them to go out and shine."

Longman says there is no such thing as a typical day. This uncertainty requires him to adapt constantly, but he doesn't mind — he loves what he does.

"As a producer, you're kind of at the heart of everything," Longman explains. The key, he says, is making sure everyone — from celebrity guests to the crew backstage — is happy. "If someone's happy, they do their best work," Longman says.

Behind the camera, Longman facilitates and manages the show's successful run. He works with writers to create skits and helps pitch ideas. Once an idea is approved, Longman oversees the final performance and editing process.

"I'm always juggling all the different sketches that we have in comedy bits," he shares.

Longman's favorite series? Crosswalk the Musical. Crosswalk sees the cast perform musical numbers amidst real-life traffic, along with celebrity guests. The filming process is just as chaotic as it sounds. Longman describes Crosswalk as "insanity over the course of a couple hours."

From Oprah to Will Smith to Tom Cruise, Longman has worked with his fair share of celebrities. But his most beloved memory is a time things didn't go as planned.

In 2017, The Late Late Show surprised an audience of 200 with the cast of Thor: Ragnarok prior to their showing. The new sketch involved a comedic, in-person performance of the movie. Longman recalls sitting hidden behind the stage podium unknowing of what would happen.

"I just remember that moment with James Corden, we kind of locked eyes and then I cued him, and he was on stage," he says. "There's moments like that where you're so far in it, you don't even know what to do."

Longman, Will Arnett and James Corden backstage.

Luckily, the skit was a success, and Longman looks back on the experience fondly. "We've got a great team here, so you're always confident it's going to be good," he says.

At home, Longman enjoys reading to his 3-year-old son, and soon, to his six-month-old newborn. He's a long way from Chigwell, yet he names childhood figures as his biggest inspirations.

He credits his parents and schoolteachers for opening his eyes to a world of endless stories; a world he hopes to pass down to his children. "I've always liked this world," he says. "I'm very lucky to work in it."

Longman with Michelle Obama.

IMAGINE:
Your book was a success! Now, it's time to bring it to the screen. How will you pitch your work to the big producers?

So far, you have:
- designed your character - inside and out
- developed your story's arc and setting
- researched your character and plot
- described your character's post-story growth

Now, all that's left is the **LOGLINE:**
a short, attention-grabbing summary.
Think of it as your hook!

Magic Formula

Protagonist + Goal + Call to Adventure + Central Conflict

IT'S YOUR TURN!

Let's use James as an example!

James dreams of becoming a big-time Hollywood producer. But his first job comes with HUGE problems - and it's his job to solve them! Will James adapt in time for his first live show?

BIG IDEAS
Lessons From Our Mentors...

1. Louis
Never give up: your childhood dreams are not silly; they are courageous.

2. Jennifer
Write stories that make you FEEL for the character. Keep practicing your craft.

3. Bruce
Our passions give us life, and even with our differences, we all BELONG.

4. Bo
Stay optimistic, passionate, and playful. Imaginations are a superpower.

5. Connie
Learning is an ADVENTURE. Don't be afraid to ask questions.

5. Amanda
Play IS learning. All of your experiences matter: they make you who you are.

6. Collette
YOU are in control of your destiny. Create the future you want for yourself.

7. James
Be positive, kind, and a good team player. Stay true to your passions.

... the possibilities are ENDLESS!

Expert Advice

Surviving School with Mike Tholfsen from Microsoft

Mike Tholfson, Principal Group Product Manager at Microsoft Education, gives his best tips and the must-have apps for surviving the school year. For more of his 'Micro Tips,' check him out on YouTube and TikTok.

By KidsRead2Kids Team

1. Hi Mike, thank you for joining us! We are big fans of your YouTube and TikTok channels (we love the Inclusive Classroom playlist!). What inspired you to start sharing your 'Micro Tips'?

During the pandemic, all these teachers were in a huge sort of desire to learn information at warp speed, because everyone had to go online, in like a week. On a whim, I made a little video to say, 'Hey, here's how to do that.' And I think on Twitter, the video had like 50,000 views. I didn't even know what a YouTube channel was.

I just sort of fiddled around and put up a few videos, and then it became kind of a pandemic hobby.

2. You've worked on over 20 Microsoft apps and platforms. Do you have a favorite?

I'd probably say OneNote. I've been a OneNote diehard for a long time. I actually worked on the OneNote team from 2004 until 2010. I was an engineering manager on the OneNote team long ago. That's probably my favorite.

3. What feature do you wish people knew more about?

Honestly, in general, the one that I wish people knew more about is the **Immersive Reader**. A lot of people use it now, but the number of people who have never heard of Immersive Reader is still stunning to me. But that one I think everyone should know about and it's made a lot of people happy and made a lot of lives easier with reading.

4. Where can we find the Immersive Reader within Microsoft products?

It's built into a lot of Microsoft products, including **Word**, **OneNote**, **Teams**, **Flipgrid**, **Forms**, **Lens**, **Whiteboard**, **Outlook**, **Edge Browser**, and **Minecraft Edu**. It's usually on the View menu of the product, depending on how the product is structured.

5. Many kids with learning differences struggle to manage assignments. Between your job, YouTube, and TikTok, how do you manage your deadlines?

It's a good question. People have asked me that before too. They're like, 'How do you keep track of all this stuff you got going on?' I have a system of productivity that I put in place for myself. It's usually a combination of Outlook and OneNote.

OneNote is great for having all your stuff organized and there are lots of different tools you can use to manage deadlines. I also like Outlook because universal for all my stuff.

When you get any job, there are other people who you depend on for deadlines too. It's not just you. You have to manage other people's deadlines with your own. So, I have a system where, if there is something important that I need, I will track what I need from the other person too.

Also, if you get asked the same questions a lot, I templatized stuff that I'm always sending the same answers to over and over again. There are ways you can do that like within seconds, versus three minutes every single time.

8. What app or product would you recommend for students in school?

So, remember, I told you my favorite program is OneNote, right? Another thing that I worked on is called **OneNote Live Captions**.

Microsoft Translator is a free tool for phones and mobile devices. So, let's say you're a student, and your teacher wants to give you an accommodation.

The teacher can get this free app called **Translator** for their phone. So basically, the teacher generates a QR code or a five-digit code, the student opens up OneNote, and there's this thing called OneNote Live Captions. Once you've accessed that, you can enter the QR code that the teacher gave you.

Everything the teacher is saying starts captioning in real-time, and you can translate in over 100 languages. You can pause the captions, highlight it, make the text bigger, hit play again, and it'll catch you back up. When it's done, it will automatically save that page into your OneNote binder.

Because OneNote has audio recording already built-in, you can take your notes out loud. We're working to roll it out to Mac and iPad, this fall as well.

9. What advice would you give to kids who dream of working with Microsoft?

It depends. For engineering, there's obviously computer science and computer engineering. But for product management, like I'm in, computer engineering is a good one.

You need a really solid, understanding of the fundamentals of how computer systems work. So computer engineering or software engineering can be useful.

But also there's the customer side and really understanding problem-solving and working with customers. A lot of what we do is talking to customers and looking for patterns. It's not black and white. Whatever industry you're really interested in, learn a lot about it.

There's so much you can learn just by digging deep into the industry and learning things like, 'Who are the top influencers? What are the top products?' A lot of times, especially for the smaller and medium-sized companies, they'll appreciate that a lot.

If you not only know about these things, you have a perspective and you have thoughts about it. Being able to talk coherently about whatever industry that you're interested in, is useful.

Persistence is also a big one. But it takes a ton of work and persistence and getting told no 1000 times. If you give up after they say no three times, then you didn't try hard enough.

10. Lastly, were you a big reader growing up? Did you have a favorite book or author?

When I was growing up, I read a lot of science fiction. I was a big Ray Bradbury fan. My dad was a science fiction person.

The Benefits of Reading Aloud

Faith Borkowsky, founder of High Five Literacy and Academic Coaching, emphasizes the importance of reading aloud.

By Faith Borkowsky

You came home from work, made dinner, cleaned up the kitchen, and now it is time to get your child to bed. If you are the parent of a child who is at least eight years old, you might just say, "Good Night!" The last thing you want to do is begin reading a book to your elementary-aged child. After all, he needs to know how to read for himself, right?

Actually, a child in the intermediate grades needs you to read aloud more than you could imagine.

"Reading aloud to a child is not just a bedtime ritual; it is one of the best ways to ensure that a child will want to read independently."

Here are **five reasons** to continue to read aloud to your child for as long as possible:

1. Vocabulary Knowledge

Conversations usually do not include academic language. The types of words used in books are not necessarily the words that a child will hear in spoken language.

"If your child is only able to read simplistic books, he will miss out on building the rich vocabulary required to succeed in school. Try chapter books that you think he may like but cannot read for himself."

Typically, your child is given leveled books in school based on his present reading ability. By reading aloud to your child a book that is beyond what he can handle on his own, you will enrich his vocabulary while he develops his reading skills.

2. Background Knowledge

A child will be able to comprehend much more of what he reads if he has a broad base of information about the world. By reading aloud to your child, you give him vicarious experiences that will help him understand content across the curriculum.

When we learn different subjects in school, we try to store what we learn in memory. We attach meaning to concepts we have heard before. This information can be filed away in our "mental file cabinets" if we already have a place to put it.

Essentially, the read-aloud is your child's first level of exposure to understanding multiple topics.

Science and social studies will make much more sense if your child has a foundation of knowledge and academic vocabulary. Frequently, "comprehension" difficulties are really just a lack of core knowledge about a subject.

3. Fluency

By modeling fluent reading, your child will begin to see that it is important to pay attention to punctuation. When a child is learning to read, it is difficult for him to decode the words AND pay attention to meaning at the same time.

Have you noticed your child reading choppily, speeding up at different moments when the words come easily but slowing down when the words are challenging?

"This is especially true with a struggling older reader. As text becomes more difficult, your child may try to juggle too many issues at the same time."

Working memory may become overloaded and fluency will suffer. If you struggle to read and feel you cannot model fluent reading, try to get audiobooks and listen to the stories together. Ask questions and have a discussion about some of the salient points.

4. Reading is a Priority

Children take cues from the people closest to them. If you continue to read aloud to your child, you send a message loud and clear that reading is important.

Just telling your child to read sends the wrong message, one that might be interpreted simply as, "You are in school, not me. If you HAVE TO READ, then go and read."

It becomes yet another chore in the household and something that is not valued.

"By making time to read together, you demonstrate how important it is to you. Each time you share a book, you are showing your child you care about reading, and you care that he becomes a reader."

5. Independence

Believe it or not, your child will become more equipped to make decisions about books and will choose to read for enjoyment more often than a child who did not get the benefit of read-alouds.

Your child will become confident about picking up lengthy books and develop the endurance to stick with them. If he only reads short, easy-to-read books, he may become intimidated and not try to read more meaty books.

"Your daily sessions will show that it may take time to complete a denser book, but it is certainly worth it.

Television shows and movies supply instant gratification while a book is meant to be visualized and taken in at a different pace. "

Faith Borkowsky is the founder of High Five Literacy and Academic Coaching with over thirty years of experience in education. Ms. Borkowsky is a Certified Dyslexia Practitioner and the author of the award-winning book, Failing Students or Failing Schools? A Parent's Guide to Reading Instruction and Intervention.

"When you read aloud to your child, you are building habits that last a lifetime."

Keep Calm and Conference On

Amanda Morin, Former Senior Expert at Understood.org, gives her advice on parent-teacher conferences.

By Amanda Morin, Neurodivergent Neurodiversity Consultant and Author

Talking to my child's teacher should be easy for me. After all, I'm a former teacher, education writer, and mom of three children ranging in age from 10 to 24 years old. I know what it's like to be the teacher who is nervous about starting a potentially difficult conversation with a parent, and what it's like to be the teacher who is delighted to be sharing great news.

I also have about 20 years of experience participating in parent-teacher conferences for my own kids.

> I know that working with the teacher can give me a fuller understanding about anything that's happening in class that I may not be seeing at home.

And as an expert, I can point to research that shows that **partnerships between schools and families** can improve students' grades, attendance, persistence, and motivation. And I can share neuroscience studies that back up that **having a good relationship with a teacher** has a positive effect on students' brains.

(How cool is that? When kids connect well with teachers, it can actually change the way their brain works.)

I've written books, articles, and worksheets to help families prepare to have meetings with teachers and to help teachers prepare to have meetings with families.

Yet, despite all of my experience and knowledge, when parent-teacher conference time rolls around, my nerves kick in. It's not easy to start the conversation or anticipate where it might go. So, I try to remember my own advice. **Here are my top tips for parent-teacher conference prep:**

1. Touch base with your child.

It's easy to overlook the fact that when it really comes down to it, parent-teacher conferences are about your child's experience in school.

So, it's important to know from your child how things are going. If your school doesn't do student-led conferences, make sure to talk to your child ahead of time. **Ask how school is going and if there's anything your child would like you to discuss with the teacher.**

2. Get your thoughts in order.

Conferences tend to be about 20 minutes long. That's not a lot of time, so gathering your thoughts ahead of time can help maximize it. Think through what you want to make sure the teacher knows.

For example: Are there things that are helping your child thrive or things that are more of a struggle? Has your family gone through any big changes that could help the teacher understand your child better?

3. Put it on paper.

Make a bulleted list of the thoughts and questions you'd like to cover, prioritized in order of importance. You may even want to share your list with the teacher before your conference to help guide the conversation.

It can help you both remember what you wanted to talk about if the conversation veers off track. But don't worry if you don't get to everything, especially if the track you veered onto is productive. If you still have things to discuss, you can ask about finding a time to continue the conversation.

4. Set the tone.

Parent-teacher conferences can get emotional, especially if your child has some struggles in school. Let the teacher know that you want to be able to speak openly and have a productive conversation about helping your child be successful in the classroom. That means each of you will need to respect the unique knowledge the other brings to the table.

That is sometimes easier said than done, so think through and establish your own boundaries for the conversation. If you're comfortable, you can share them with the teacher, so they become agreed-upon meeting norms. **A couple of suggestions:**

- Be respectful of time — both your own and the teacher's. Arrive on time and wrap up within the time allotted. Expect the same of the teacher.

If the meeting begins late, ask if you can run over. If that's not an option, ask to reschedule.

- Expect to be treated with respect when sharing your thoughts, and show the same respect for the teacher.

- Presume good intention. If you feel it's necessary to make that clear, explain to the teacher that you work under the assumption that everyone has the best of intentions for this discussion.

- Be open to hearing information you didn't know, even if it's uncomfortable to hear.

- Know that it's OK to say you need some time to process what you're hearing before responding and that the teacher may need to do so as well.

5. Use "I" statements.

These statements let you share your thoughts in a way that sounds less personal. It's easier to be heard when you frame what you say through your perspective. "I" sentences start with phrases like, "I noticed," "I'm worried," or "I feel."

For instance, saying, "Why do my child's essays get low grades, but you don't add comments about how to improve the writing?" may put a teacher on the defensive and shut down what could be a productive conversation.

> **Instead, you could say, "I notice that you don't provide written feedback on my child's essays. Have you spoken to my child about what needs improvement?"**

This explains your concern, shows that you're considering that feedback may have been provided already, and allows for more conversation.

6. Try to be solution-oriented.

It's easy to identify problems, but it's helpful to also come to the table with ideas for solutions. For example, if you know that taking a "brain break" every half hour helps your child focus more easily at home, suggest seeing if it works at school too.

Or, if you don't have a solution, let the teacher know you'd like to work together to find one and not just point out a concern. If you're not looking for a solution and just wanted to share information, make sure that's clear.

7. Follow up with your child.

Talking after the conference is important. It can relieve any worry your child may have had about how the conversation went. It gives you a chance to share any information related to what your child wanted you to discuss with the teacher.

It allows you to share any solutions that were talked about so your child knows what to expect. **Most of all, though, it lets your child know you're open to talking about school.**

> **My best advice, though, is something that I use as a mantra: Stay calm.**

> **Parent-teacher conferences can be nerve-racking. They can feel big and overwhelming.**

> **But I take a few deep breaths and remember that parents and teachers share a common goal. We're all just trying to provide the best learning experience for our kids.**

> Amanda Morin is a writer and senior expert at Understood, specializing in Family Advocacy and Education. She worked as a classroom teacher and an early intervention specialist for 10 years.

Mom2Mom
(and Dad!)

Welcome to Mom2Mom!

Welcome to Mom2Mom, where I will share my own personal journey as a parent, along with my best tips for success.

By Carol Blumenstein

Hi, I'm Carol Blumenstein and I am the mother of Alana, Jacob, Reuben, Julia and Benjamin. In Mom2Mom, I will share my own experience as a parent — and share my best tips as well. Let me tell you a little bit about myself and my family.

Before creating KidsRead2Kids, several of my children were bullied in school and had low self-esteem. School was a very hard place to be. By getting them involved in a project they were passionate about, they each had an opportunity to grow into the people they are today.

"Each one brought their own gifts to the website and magazine. Alana, our Editor-in-Chief, brought her love of writing. She interviews and writes the articles and reads several of our books. Jacob, our movie buff, edits our videos and creates our original music.

Reuben, our artist extraordinaire, designs our logos and all our artwork. Benjamin helps design the lesson plans and Julia takes amazing pictures."

> "You see, in the process of building KidsRead2Kids, my children were able to see their own strengths as well. My children are no longer ashamed of their learning differences. They define themselves by their strengths and not their struggles."

But helping children is not enough. Parents also need help. That is where Mom2Mom comes in. Together we can share tips, tools, and advice to help you give your child the hope and confidence they will need to succeed in life.

When I was growing up, I too struggled in school. I had a difficult time reading and spelling and often felt stupid in comparison to my classmates. Fortunately, my mom believed in me. She encouraged me to study computer programming and to get involved in community theater. With her support, I was confident in my abilities and worked hard on my studies.

At the end of my junior year of high school, I sub-matriculated into the University of Pennsylvania's M&T program. There, I duel majored in electrical engineering and finance. After working as a management consultant for Booz Allen and Bain, I received my MBA at Wharton.

Although I succeeded as a consultant and reached my career goals — the painful feelings I faced in my childhood always stuck with me.

Watching my kids go through the same experience I had as a child pushed me to be the advocate I was meant to be. Along the way, I learned countless lessons about how to empower my children. Now, I want to share them with you.

Each Mom2Mom will focus on a new way you can help your child succeed. We will also invite guest moms to share their personal experiences.

We hope to create a safe space for parents, so no parent feels alone or overwhelmed. Remember, your child's success in life goes beyond report cards.

> "It depends on a healthy sense of self, the willingness to ask for help, the determination to keep trying despite their struggles, and the ability to form healthy friendships. Success begins with confidence and self-acceptance. Success begins at home."

Your Child is NOT Broken

If you are ashamed, they will be ashamed

If you feel hopeless, they will feel hopeless

> My mother didn't view me as broken. As someone who needed to be fixed.

> She saw my strengths, my passions, and my interests, and encouraged me along the way. I am the person that I am today because of her.

The Role of Parents and Teachers...

A child's self-esteem starts with **YOU!**

It is our job to see the best in our children so that they ultimately will see the best in themselves.

Before we can build our children's confidence, we have to be confident in our children.

YOU are their MIRROR: how you feel is what they see.

Dad2Dad with Jordan Levin: The Early Years

In our very first Dad2Dad, Meet Jordan Levin, owner of Crossfit Bloomfield. Here, he shares his story of growing up deaf and ADHD.

By Jordan Levin

Have you ever heard the expression, flying by the seat of your pants? That was me. I was a very hyperactive kid growing up. I was always on the move. If Curious George could be a human, he would be named Curious Jordan.

To throw some extra spice into the mix, I was also deaf.

I didn't have any understandable speech in my early years. It wasn't until 3rd or 4th grade when anyone could begin to understand me.

Think about this, when a baby is born, they hear every single sound the second they enter the world. That means every single conversation, cooing, animal noise, house sounds, etc.

My first 2.5 years were radio silence. My audible speech arrived fashionably late to the party. This made for a very difficult time in kindergarten and elementary school.

Dedication and Consistency

At the end of each day during elementary school, my mother, armed with her notebook would talk with the teachers when she picked me up from school. We would then go home and both of my parents would go through the entire day of class again and again.

Along with my parents, I had the help of tutors sitting beside me, going over everything orally as well as on paper. This had to be repeated multiple times before I was able to retain the material.

Can you imagine how difficult that was for a young Jordan or any kid? Do you think I really wanted to do this? I just wanted to be outside with my friends.

However, I had parents who lovingly threw me in with the wolves. For the sake of my profound hearing loss they knew I had to learn to adapt, and thankfully that came easily for me.

Years later, at the age of 17, I was diagnosed with ADHD. This was such an eye-opener for me.

The first time I took medication was the first time I actually took a sincere interest in reading. To test the waters, I opened a book. Page one turned into page two which turned into page thirty-two and so on.

I was so hyper-focused on this particular book that I didn't even notice that there was a commotion going on in the background. Before this, getting me to sit and willingly read anything was virtually impossible.

I felt so smart. I was finally able to comprehend and retain what I had just read. I said to my parents, "If we knew about this earlier, I'd be in Harvard by now!"

We all knew at that moment that my strengths would get stronger but, most importantly, **my areas for improvement** might actually or COULD actually turn out to be my strengths moving forward.

Instilling Good Habits

I have come to believe that everything happens for a reason and that every speed bump is just another opportunity to create a positive impact.

It is only appropriate that being someone who happens to be profoundly deaf and who has ADHD, I am also the owner of CrossFit Bloomfield.

Movement has been a key building block in my self-esteem, my perception, and instilling a sense of gratitude.

In my current profession, we have a couple of key catchphrases: "Be comfortable with the uncomfortable," and "Be prepared for the unknown."

Each day is far from unknown. Every child is like a snowflake in the sense that the way in which they learn and retain information is just as unique as each individual. Because of that, instilling habits of positive movement can be a grounding and positive reinforcement.

I knew I was capable and able to play sports and move successfully in whatever capacity I set my mind to.

I understood that if a hockey player got put into the penalty box, the team still had to work and strategize with whomever it had left.

I realized that my body was my own team. NOTHING about me was penalized.

In fact, this was the perfect opportunity to sharpen all my other senses and acknowledge everything that I could do vs. worry about what I couldn't.

In order to be prepared for the unknown, you have to be able to tap into your other resources or in my experience, my other senses.

The positive movement that I needed to help keep me grounded as a child, is the same habit I am instilling to both children and adults as my career.

Movement - whether it be sports, yoga, dance, martial arts, or even meditation - can bring a sense of joy and stability to any child.

Instilling positive habits is like giving a child a home base to land. **Land with gratitude. Land with mindfulness. Land with purpose.**

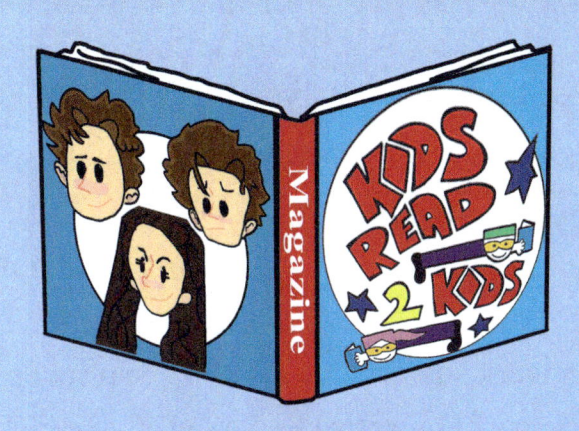

Either write something worth **READING,**

or do something worth **WRITING.**

Benjamin Franklin

5 Tips to Help Your Dyslexic Child with Homework

Educator and attorney Nicole Holcomb founded Dyslexia Mom Life, a podcast for parents of children with dyslexia.

DYSLEXIA Mom Life with Nicole Holcomb

For many moms (me included) raising children with dyslexia, homework is their least favorite part of their day. **But, it doesn't have to be that way.**

Children with dyslexia work so hard at school. Our children know at an early age that their classmates are able to read, write, and spell with ease. By the time our kids get home from school, they are mentally and physically exhausted. They just want to rest, reset, and recharge. But, here we come with the backpack... and the battle begins. The homework battle.

When you have a plan to train for a marathon (yep, homework is the long game), then you will find more daily success. If you just wing it, then you and your child will be more frustrated with homework. No one wants that.

These five tips will make homework manageable for you and your child!

1. Get your homework space ready.

Why help set up the homework space? Well, if your child uses the little bit of energy they have left getting their backpack out, pulling out homework, finding a pencil, then looking for their agenda . . . well, you will either have a child procrastinating or frustrated trying to find his agenda, pencil, homework folder, etc.

Will there be a time when your child will be able to get organized for homework? Yes, that is the ultimate goal. But, you know your child and know when they are ready. We are trying to reduce anxiety and frustration before homework begins.

2. Review the homework and decide how much help to provide.

Take a few minutes to look over the homework. **What needs to be done that night? Where will you need to provide the most support?** Are there any tests or projects due in the next week that need to be spread out over the week?

Read the instructions to your child and ask them to explain what needs to be done. **Be available to help. Be patient. Be present.**

3. Let your child decide where to start.

Ask your child what they would like to start on first. You can talk about what assignments must be completed that night, including work on projects and studying for tests. This will provide your child with the opportunity for decision-making and a little control over the homework.

4. Take a break and get moving.

When your child is pushing back on homework, I have found the best thing to do is give a short break. Get your child up and moving. This will get their brain ready to focus again.

Be sure to set a timer and let your child know how long of a break they can have before getting back to the homework. If you feel yourself losing your patience, this is a good time to check-in with yourself. This may be a good time for you to take a few deep breaths too.

5. Decide when it's time to be done.

You are your child's best advocate. If it's time to call the homework done, then call it! The teacher may not realize your child is spending an hour on an assignment that should have taken 15 minutes, according to the teacher. If your child is too tired to read, then read to them or have an audiobook for her. There are always options to help her practice skills.

For some kiddos, they prefer to do homework in the mornings before school when they are fresh and rested. If your child is having trouble with fatigue at night, change the time of day and see if that helps.

Your child may not remember you pushing them to finish their second grade math homework, but they will remember your compassion, patience, and support. The goal is to not sacrifice your relationship with your child over homework. You got this!

Amazing Tales
Hunt for the answers as you read!

Across

3. Listening is the SAME as reading! That's why we love listening to **AUDIOBOOKS**.
8. What is Jacob's favorite book? **AWRINKLEINTIME**
10. Bruce Lanoil plays **PRETEND** for a living.
11. What is Alana's superpower? **EMPATHY**
12. According to American Girl's Jennifer Hirsch, all stories have a beginning, middle, and end. Or, an **ARC**.
15. In Tips From Us, we encourage **ACTIVE** listening.
17. How many flavors does Collette's cookie company have? **SIX**
21. For those struggling to read, try **HIGHINTEREST**, low-level books.
22. Where is Aarav from? **SINGAPORE**
23. Who is Louis Henry Mitchell's favorite Sesame Street Muppet? **COOKIEMONSTER**
24. Literacy expert Faith Borkowsky emphasizes the importance of **READING** aloud.

Down

1. Siena Castellon is changing the **NARRATIVE** on learning challenges.
2. Our mission is to bring the joy, **CONFIDENCE**, and curiosity back to all readers.
4. Bo Stjerne Thomsen is the VP of Learning Through Play at the LEGO **FOUNDATION**.
5. What makes you different makes you **SPECIAL**.
6. What is Benjamin's favorite book? **THELIGHTNINGTHIEF**
7. What is our nonprofit called? **KIDSREAD2KIDS**
9. To live a balanced life, we must focus on diet, sleep, and **EXERCISE**.
10. Amanda Gummer credits **PLAY** for her success.
13. What exploding craft do we make in Ready. Set. STEM? **VOLCANO**
14. What book does our volunteer Steven read? **PETERPAN**
16. What is Benjamin's superpower? **CURIOSITY**
18. What record-breaking LEGO ship did Brynjar build? **TITANIC**
19. Mike Tholfsen of Microsoft Education loves giving his **MICRO** tips.
20. Where is Brynjar from? **ICELAND**

VOCABULARY

Our Favorite Words From Our Book!

VOCABULARY

Our favorite vocabulary from Steven (see page 65)! Using your KR2K Word Jar, write down each new word.

Imaginative	**ADJECTIVE** — Inventive and original	"I thought that it was so imaginative and so fun and so creative."
Fearless	**ADJECTIVE** — Brave and courageous	"I just remember being so inspired by … how fearless they were."
Transport	**VERB** — Take or carry from one place to another	"I loved the ability to transport myself into another world…"
Immerse	**VERB** — To be captured by an activity or interest	"…and to just be … immersed in another character's life."
Unleash	**VERB** — To let loose or begin something powerful	"That really allowed me to unleash my creativity."

Flair	**NOUN** Special talent or individual style	"I really liked that it was me, and it had my own flair."
Determination	**NOUN** Overcoming obstacles to achieve a goal	"I used to struggle … with determination and focus."
Adaptive	**ADJECTIVE** Ability to adjust to change	"They raised … their kids with such grace, and they were … adaptive."
Curve-ball	**NOUN** Something surprising or unexpected	"I threw my parents many curve-balls growing up."
Regardless	**ADVERB** Despite everything	"They love me regardless."
Diligent	**ADJECTIVE** Showing constant care and effort	"They are incredibly diligent workers. They love giving 100%."

Dedicate	**VERB** Devote time and effort to a task	"She just dedicated herself: no matter what."
Compassion	**NOUN** Caring about others and wanting to help	"I would certainly change how much compassion … people have."
Empathy	**NOUN** Understanding another's feelings and point-of-view	"And empathy… sometimes we forget to put ourselves in the shoes of others."
Perspective	**NOUN** A way of seeing something; a point-of-view	"Try to shift your perspective on reading… look at it as something fun."
Genre	**NOUN** A category or style	"Find your genre of books that you will fall in love with."
Intrigue	**VERB** To interest or fascinate	"Say… 'This really intrigues me; do you have any books that you would recommend?'."

VOCABULARY

Our favorite vocabulary from Aarav (see page 72)! Using your KR2K Word Jar, write down each new word.

Word	Definition	Example
Singapore	**NOUN** An island country in Southeast Asia, meaning, "Lion City"	"I have been in Singapore for over 5 years now."
Opportunity	**NOUN** A chance or possibility	"I also got an opportunity to read for the National Library Board of Singapore."
Defeat	**NOUN** The loss of a contest or failure to win	"I had a hard time accepting defeat at any games I played with my friends."
Forgive	**VERB** To let go of a past hurt or offense	"I also forgive very quickly, I hope it counts as a superpower."
Pollution	**NOUN** Harmful materials in the environment	"I don't like water pollution."

VOCABULARY

Our favorite vocabulary from Brynjar (see page 78)! Using your KR2K Word Jar, write down each new word.

Replica	**NOUN** An exact copy or model of something	"Brynjar was just ten when he built the 26-foot-long replica."
Charming	**ADJECTIVE** Polite, friendly, and likeable	"At 17, he is charming, expressive, and kind."
Expressive	**ADJECTIVE** Showing feelings, easy to read	"At 17, he is charming, expressive, and kind."
Mission	**NOUN** An important goal or purpose	"… with a big heart and a mission to help others."
Campaign	**NOUN** A plan to acheive a goal	"Brynjar's big dream soon went viral — all thanks to a Kickstarter campaign."

Word	Part of Speech / Definition	Example
Accumulate	VERB — To gather together or increase an amount	"His video … asked the public if they could help him "accumulate 56 thousand Lego cubes.""
Feature	VERB — To have as an important participant	"Brynjar was featured on Discovery Science, CBS News, and other major channels."
Autism	NOUN — A different kind of brain development	"Today, Brynjar is proudest of his journey with autism."
Engage	VERB — To participate or become involved	"His social skills have greatly improved, allowing him to engage in conversations."
Attract	VERB — To captivate, charm, or fascinate	"He wasn't able to attract kids."
Diagnose	VERB — To identify the cause of symptoms	"Brynjar was five years old when he was first diagnosed."

Develop	**VERB** — To grow and mature	"When they're allowed to develop through their interest, something sparks."
Spark	**VERB** — To ignite (an interest or passion)	"When they're allowed to develop through their interest, something sparks."
Premiere	**NOUN** — The first showing or opening	"Brynjar's documentary … premiered in April 2021."
Target	**NOUN** — The aim of an attack or goal	"'I want to become a captain,' Brynjar says. 'That's my next target.'"
Ambition	**NOUN** — A strong desire to achieve something	"He's aware that it's a big ambition."
Contrary	**NOUN** — The opposite	"But Brynjar isn't worried. On the contrary, he believes in himself."

VOCABULARY

Our favorite vocabulary from Siena (see page 84)! Using your KR2K Word Jar, write down each new word.

Word	Type & Definition	Example
Narrative	NOUN — A story, POV, or account of events	"Castellon aims to change the narrative on neurodiversity."
Mentor	NOUN — A role model or teacher	"She hoped to provide empowering … mentorship for kids like her."
Sprinkle	NOUN — A small amount scattered somewhere	"Castellon spent hours searching … finding sprinkles here and there."
Epiphany	NOUN — A moment of realization	"One day, she had an epiphany."
Reject	VERB — To dismiss or refuse	"When it comes to bullies, the best thing to do is reject their view entirely."

Limited	**ADJECTIVE** Short, small, or restricted	"They felt limited by the outside world."
Misconception	**NOUN** An incorrect view or opinion	"Unfortunately, misconceptions like these are everywhere."
Recognize	**VERB** To show appreciation, affection, or respect	"The program … encourages schools to recognize and celebrate neurodiverse students."
Game-changer	**NOUN** Something new that causes great change	"Her book, which was a game-changer for autistic girls, is another."
Distinction	**NOUN** A difference or contrast	"'Make a distinction between what's helpful and what's harmful.'"
Utilize	**VERB** To make practical use of something	"To become a changemaker, Castellon suggests utilizing social media."

Advocacy	**NOUN** — The act of supporting a cause	"Her advocacy is stronger because she's able to connect with her audience."
Celebrate	**VERB** — To appreciate, honor, or praise	"Castellon happily celebrates her differences."
Neurodiversity	**NOUN** — Having a brain that works differently than the standard	"Thanks to her neurodiversity, Castellon is an excellent problem solver."
Lens	**NOUN** — An individual perspective	"[Siena] sees the world through a unique lens."
Conquer	**VERB** — To successfully overcome a problem	"Castellon has conquered nearly every problem."
Gratitude	**NOUN** — The quality of being thankful	"She feels nothing but gratitude for her journey."

VOCABULARY

Our favorite vocabulary from Jennifer Hirsch (see page 140)! Using your KR2K Word Jar, write down each new word.

Word	Part of Speech / Definition	Example
Trough	**NOUN** — A long, narrow open container for animals to feed out of	"I have … 16 huge goldfish that live in an old cattle trough."
Catalogue	**NOUN** — A complete list of items	"I read all the … catalogues, finding and fixing errors."
Illustrate	**VERB** — To create visuals, drawings or pictures	"I began to write and illustrate stories for fun."
Sculpt	**VERB** — To shape, mold, or carve a figure out of a hard material	"I wrote poetry and learned clay sculpting."
Plausible	**ADJECTIVE** — Reasonable or believable	"I'll help the author … make it fun, interesting, and plausible."

Word	Part of Speech / Definition	Example
Accurate	**ADJECTIVE** Correct in all details; exact	"I meet with … our historian, who makes sure that everything is accurate."
Trendy	**ADJECTIVE** Fashionable or up to date	"The 1980s are trendy because it's the era many parents grew up in."
Inspire	**VERB** To motivate, encourage, or breathe life into	"Many of Julie's experiences were inspired by things that happened."
Conflict	**NOUN** A struggle, opposition, or clash of opinion	"The main character must solve the conflict in a convincing way."
Essential	**ADJECTIVE** Absolutely necessary and important	"It's essential to respect your audience."
Honesty	**NOUN** The quality of being fair, truthful, and sincere	"I look for children's authors who write with intelligence and honesty."

Channel	**VERB** To express or communicate	"... and who can 'channel' a child's voice and viewpoint."
Arc	**NOUN** The plot of the story, from beginning to end	"To create a story arc, you need a beginning, middle, and end."
Protagonist	**NOUN** The main character of a story	"The main character, or protagonist, must change from beginning to end."
Greedy	**ADJECTIVE** Selfish, wanting more than what is fair	"For example: In A Christmas Carol, Scrooge starts out greedy and selfish."
Vow	**VERB** To solemnly promise	"He vows to change his ways."
Generous	**ADJECTIVE** Giving, willing to help	"The final scene shows how Scrooge has changed to become generous and caring."

VOCABULARY

Our favorite vocabulary from Bruce Lenoil (see page 152)! Using your KR2K Word Jar, write down each new word.

Adventure	**NOUN** — An exciting trip or experience	"Bruce Lanoil's imagination took him on countless adventures."
Beloved	**ADJECTIVE** — Adored, idolized, and admired	"Lanoil's performances ... bring to life beloved characters."
Manifest	**VERB** — To turn an idea into reality	"'All of these things that I saw as a kid, unbelievably, I manifested in my life.'"
Emigrate	**VERB** — To leave one's country and settle in another	"'All my dad's parents emigrated, and so they were trying to fit in.'"
Humor	**NOUN** — The quality of being amusing or funny	"'I found everybody's sense of humor.'"

Word	Part of Speech / Definition	Example
Defuse	VERB — To reduce the danger or tension	"'I defused a lot of situations...'"
Inject	VERB — To introduce something	"'... by seeing where I could inject something lighter for everybody.'"
Impression	NOUN — An idea, feeling, or opinion about someone	"Kids made first-glance impressions."
Cherish	VERB — To protect and care for lovingly	"But the friends he made, he cherished for life."
Contemplate	VERB — To think about or consider	"Lanoil contemplated quitting."
Confined	ADJECTIVE — Limited or restricted	"'I wasn't confined by what you saw, because I could do anything.'"

Improvisation	**NOUN** Ad-libbing dialogue in the moment	"... learning useful skills like improvisation."
Coordination	**NOUN** The ability to smoothly use parts of the body	"... and strengthening his hand-eye coordination."
Interconnected	**ADJECTIVE** Linked or related to one another	"'Then you understand ... how we are interconnected.'"
United	**ADJECTIVE** Joined together for a common purpose	"'Everybody in the audience was united.'"
Despondent	**ADJECTIVE** In low spirits from loss of hope or courage	"The group seemed utterly despondent."
Ensemble	**NOUN** A group that performs together	"This ensemble, who are just grown men playing their hearts out.'"

VOCABULARY

Our favorite vocabulary from Bo Stjerne Thomsen (see page 158)! Using your KR2K Word Jar, write down each new word.

Stimuate	**VERB** Encourage interest or activity	"'My parents ... provide access to stimulation in the environment.'"
Wander	**VERB** To walk without direction	"The freedom to wander ... allowed him infinite opportunities to use his imagination."
Wonder	**VERB** To be curious or amazed	"The freedom to wander (and wonder) allowed him ... to use his imagination."
Evidence	**NOUN** Facts that prove something is true	"'I collect ... evidence ... on how children learn through playful experiences.'"
Inform	**VERB** To give someone facts or information	"'I help inform our decisions around what kind of activities to do.'"

Invention	**NOUN** — A new thing created by someone	" … the creative workspace behind several of their key … inventions."
Evaluate	**VERB** — To determine the quality or value	"'When we do this, we are not only creating, but also evaluating.'"
Infinite	**ADJECTIVE** — Limitless or endless	"There's an infinite number of ways to express your ideas."
Meaningful	**ADJECTIVE** — Having a purpose or importance	"'It's really about … expressing ideas that are meaningful to you.'"
Stigma	**NOUN** — A set of negative beliefs	"Thomsen's aware of the stigma behind play."
Frivolous	**ADJECTIVE** — Having no serious purpose or value	"'I think sometimes we think about play as something … frivolous.'"

Inherent	**ADJECTIVE** Being a part of the nature of a person or thing	"'It's so inherently serious, because you actually develop confidence.'"
Passionate	**ADJECTIVE** Having very strong feelings about something	"'You have been doing projects that you're passionate about.'"
Collaborate	**VERB** To work with others on a task	"'You get more creative and collaborative at the same time.'"
Experiential	**ADJECTIVE** Learning by exploring, creating, experiencing, and discovering	"... he says of interactive, experiential learning."
Optimism	**NOUN** Hopefulness and positivity about the future	"'I think it's very important to keep that optimism.'"
Undefined	**ADJECTIVE** Not clearly shown; unlimited	"Create your own life, undefined by who other people think you are."

Thank you so much for supporting us! Visit us at KidsRead2Kids.com. Happy Reading! :)

Follow us using the QR code.

© 2016-2024 KidsRead2Kids. All Rights Reserved.

Our Resources

Video-Audiobooks
A collection of 16 Classic Novels, Decodable Chapter Books, and Early Learner Read-Alouds.

Lesson Plans
Listening comprehension questions, creative writing prompts, and fun games for each chapter.

Private Tutoring
Together, we'll study anything from reading to essay writing to executive functioning.

Parent Coaching
Our Parent Founder Carol is here to help you empower your child to be a strong, independent learner.

Classes + Curriculum

Intro to Journalism
6 sessions, ages 12 and up. Learn to write a Book Review, Q&A, and Feature Article. Finished pieces will have the opportunity to be published in KidsRead2Kids Magazine.

Private Reading
Includes reading of chosen story by a KidsRead2Kids Co-Founder and some fun discussion questions. (For a longer novel, repurchase to continue reading!)

Intro to Poetry
Ages 8-12, 3 private 50-minute sessions. Have fun learning to write poetry, with the chance of being published in KidsRead2Kids Magazine.

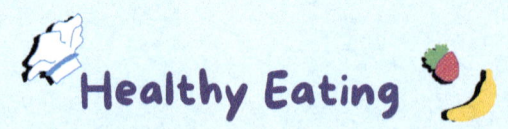

The Poetry Corner

Healthy Eating
Our healthy eating seminar teaches the key components of a balanced diet. Plus, cook with us! Learn fun, energy boosting recipes for the whole family.

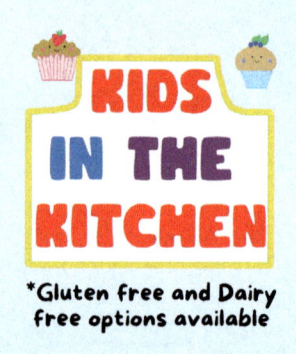

KIDS IN THE KITCHEN
Gluten free and Dairy free options available

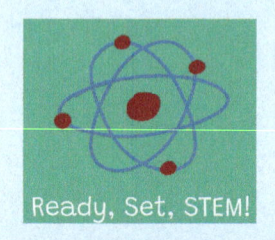

Ready, Set, STEM!
Learn science through FUN, interactive activities like our edible play-dough, slime, exploding volcanoes, and more!

Multisensory Book Club
We Make Learning FUN!

KidsRead2Kids Book Club provides hands-on, pedagogy-backed learning experiences to help children become independent, lifelong learners. Each child is paired with a high school mentor, who serves as a positive Reading Role Model. Club meetings consist of a book, read interactively to encourage engagement, and a unique activity designed to teach something new.

The Worry Box
Meet Felix, the Worry Monster:

he's designed to hold all your worries, big and small. Our Worry Box teaches children to recognize their feelings, and uses origami to turn them into something beautiful.

*Mini Monster Puppets

The Word Jar
A Collection of Words as Unique As You Are

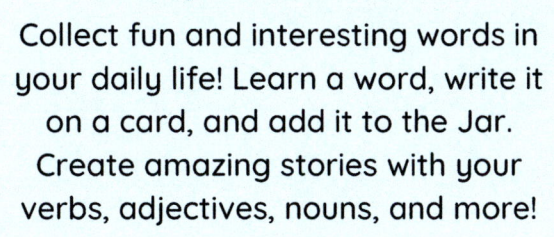

Collect fun and interesting words in your daily life! Learn a word, write it on a card, and add it to the Jar. Create amazing stories with your verbs, adjectives, nouns, and more!

The Bear Hunt
An interactive extravaganza!

Set up anywhere for a day of sleuthing fun! Turn your home, library, or even your town into a bear themed learning hunt, complete with a special certificate for all who partake!

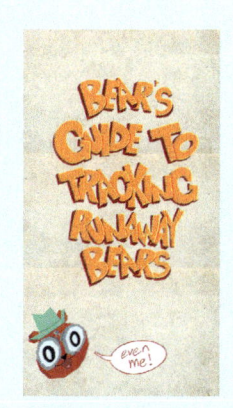

Printed in Great Britain
by Amazon